A QUESTION O

EMLYN HUGHES

A QUESTION OF CRICKET

AN ARTHUR BARKER QUIZ BOOK

Arthur Barker
A division of George Weidenfeld and Nicolson Limited
London

Acknowledgements

I would like to thank Peter Wynne-Thomas, the archivist at Trent Bridge and the Secretary of the Association of Cricket Statisticians, and Michael Newell for all their help in compiling these questions.

PICTURE CREDITS

The photographs in this book were provided by the following:

Patrick Eagar 4, 9, 12; *Interaction* 11; *Sport & General* 7; *Trent Bridge Archive* 3; *Weidenfeld Archive* 1, 2, 5, 6, 8, 9, 10.

Cover photographs by *Colin Thomas*.

Published in Great Britain by
George Weidenfeld & Nicolson Limited
91 Clapham High Street
London SW4 7TA

Photoset by Deltatype, Ellesmere Port

Printed in Great Britain by
The Guernsey Press Co. Ltd., Guernsey, C. I.

INTRODUCTION

The questions in this book are specially arranged in categories, marked A–J as follows:

A *Test Cricket* – cricket and cricketers at the highest level.

B *Grounds and Venues* – incidents which are remembered because of their location as well as the cricketers involved.

C *First-Class English Cricket* – happenings in the County Championship.

D *Bowlers* – fast, slow and medium, their facts and feats.

E *Batsmen* – famous innings remembered, odd dismissals recalled.

F *In the Field* – wicketkeepers and fielders and the laws of the game.

G *The One Day Game* – the excitement of the cup finals at Lord's, the World Cup and Sunday League cricket.

H *Captains* – how they succeeded and indeed how they failed to lead their team to victory.

I *The History of the Game* – what do you know of the game as recalled by your father and even by your grandfather.

J *Joker* – odd quirks and incidents.

With this system, the quizzes can not only be tackled head on as they come (1–65, A–J), or category by category (quizzes made up exclusively of 'D', 'F' or 'G' questions, etc.), but also on a selective basis with players choosing questions by category preference rather than proceeding in straight sequence A–J.

Most questions, except in category 'I', relate to the post-1945 period and the vast majority of questions, except of course those in Test and one-day internationals, relate to cricket in England. All records are up to date to the completion of England's tour to New Zealand in March 1988.

The answers conform to the Guides to First-Class Cricket issued by the Association of Cricket Statisticians.

FOREWORD

Anyone who has flicked through the records section of *Wisden Cricketers' Almanack* will know that there are endless questions that can be asked about cricket. And what's more, in the average English summer, there's plenty of time to ask them when rain stops play. So next time you're staring morosely out of the pavilion window or waiting for coverage to resume on the telly, get out this quiz book and ask your friends *A Question of Cricket*.

Howzat!

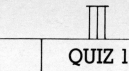

QUIZ 1

ANSWERS ON PAGE 79

A Name the body that controls world cricket.

B Which present Football League ground was once the venue of Test cricket?

C Which county won the County Championship for the first time in 1961?

D Whose leg-spin confused England in 1987–88?

E Who hit the most sixes in an English first-class season?

F He came out of retirement to act as substitute wicketkeeper for England in a Test in 1986. Who was he?

G Which England batsman was dismissed on 99 in the one-day international at The Oval in 1986?

H Which batsman captained England in twenty-three post-war Tests, but was never appointed captain of his county side?

I For which county did the immortal W.G. Grace play?

J What did Dennis Lillee say to the Queen during the 1977 Centenary Test at Melbourne.

QUIZ 2

ANSWERS ON PAGE 79

A   Which two countries toured England in the summer of 1986?

B   Which major English county ground has a tree within the boundary?

C   What fundamental change was introduced to first-class County Championship cricket in 1988?

D   Which bowler was nicknamed 'Typhoon'?

E   Who had a batting average exceeding 100 in two first-class English seasons?

F   Who, in 1979–80, was the first wicketkeeper to make ten dismissals in a Test match?

G   Who were the first winners of the NatWest Trophy?

H   Which brothers both captained Australia during the last twenty years?

I   Name the small Hampshire village, known as the 'Cradle of Cricket', due to its famous eighteenth-century cricket team?

J   What did Malcolm Marshall and Paul Terry do in common during the 1984 England vs West Indies Test series?

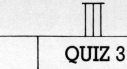

QUIZ 3

ANSWERS ON PAGE 80

A   Which Worcestershire cricketer made his Test début for New Zealand in 1986–87?

B   Where is the Kirkstall Lane End?

C   For which county did Jack Robertson create a record Championship score of 331 not out in 1949?

D   Which bowler lost four toes while touring the West Indies with England in 1967–68?

E   Who reached his 100th first-class hundred in 1986?

F   England wicketkeeper Roy Swetman represented no less than three counties – for which one was he playing when he appeared for his country?

G   Scotland have only beaten one side in the Benson & Hedges Cup – which was it?

H   Which Warwickshire player briefly replaced Clive Lloyd as captain of the West Indies' Test team?

I   Have eight ball overs ever been used in English County Championship cricket?

J   Why would Derek Underwood be pleased to find a sticky dog?

QUIZ 4

ANSWERS ON PAGE 80

A In 1982 which cricketer decided to play for England in a Test rather than in the university match?

B Where did Notts play 'home' matches outside their county boundary in the 1980s?

C Home many counties take part in the County Championship?

D Jim Laker and Tony Lock were two Surrey bowlers to represent England in the 1950s, who was the third Surrey bowler, whose surname also begins with 'L', to play for England around this time?

E Who scored a triple hundred in county cricket in 1985?

F Which wicketkeeper played in 412 consecutive Championship matches for Yorkshire between 1955 and 1969?

G Two New Zealanders have taken 100 wickets in one-day internationals. Richard Hadlee is one, name the other.

H Which father and son captained India in post-war Tests?

I Did India or the West Indies make their bow in Test match cricket first?

J George Davis had a dramatic effect on the Leeds Test match of 1975, though he was not present and is unknown to cricketing fame. What occurred?

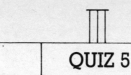

QUIZ 5

ANSWERS ON PAGE 81

A Name the three Middlesex players to captain England in the 1980s?

B Name the ground now used by Glamorgan in Cardiff.

C The County Championship is sponsored by Britannic Assurance, which company previously acted as sponsors?

D Which bowler was the cause of the 1980–81 Test between England and West Indies at Georgetown being cancelled?

E Which batsman hit 312 not out for MCC at Peshawar in 1966–67 and later captained England?

F Which England wicketkeeper was Secretary for MCC from 1962 to 1974?

G In a one-day Sunday League match, how many fielders must be inside the 30 yard circle?

H Which West Indies captain was knighted in 1964?

I Which present first-class county was the last to join the County Championship?

J Can you name the Scotsman, the Welshman and the South African who captained England in the 1970s?

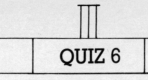

QUIZ 6

ANSWERS ON PAGE 82

A   Which two countries compete for the Wisden Trophy?

B   Who plays on May's Bounty?

C   Which English seaside town holds a 'Cricket festival' each September, involving first-class cricket?

D   Who was Alf Valentine's famous spinning partner of the 1950s?

E   Which famous Indian batsman played for Somerset in 1980?

F   Who was the reserve West Indian wicketkeeper on their 1984 tour of England?

G   Which country that does not play Test cricket took part in the 1987–88 World Cup?

H   Who led the Rest of the World in the Bicentenary Match at Lord's in 1987?

I   Where was the first Test match staged?

J   Which fictional first-class cricketer was a jewel thief?

QUIZ 7

ANSWERS ON PAGE 82

A All the overseas countries bar one played their initial Test match against England. Name the exception.

B Where was the first tied Test match staged?

C Name the official body which governs first-class county cricket in England?

D Which pair of fast bowlers came to England and helped win the Ashes for Australia in 1948?

E Which elegant post-war English batsman has the christian names Peter Barker Howard?

F Which wicketkeeper moved from Surrey to Sussex in 1975–76?

G What is the record for economical bowling in Sunday League cricket?

H Whom did Ian Greig succeed as captain of Surrey in 1987?

I Lord Hawke and Lord Harris were both influential figures in cricket administration, having earlier been county captains – of which counties?

J What metal object upset Mike Brearley in Perth in 1979?

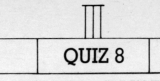

QUIZ 8

ANSWERS ON PAGE 83

A Why did no Test matches take place in England in 1970?

B Which Test ground was founded by William Clarke?

C For which counties have rugby full-backs, Dusty Hare and Alistair Hignell played cricket?

D In 1987 who were Leicestershire's two overseas fast bowlers?

E What is curious about the first-class career of batsman Roger Knight?

F Of which player did Richie Benaud say that his idea of setting a field was to say: 'OK fellas, scatter!'?

G What is the name of Australia's one-day inter-state competition?

H Who captained the rebel Australian team to South Africa in 1985 and 1986?

I Who was Jack Hobbs's famous England batting partner in the latter part of Hobbs's career?

J What unfortunate fate do Andy Ganteaume and Rodney Redmond share?

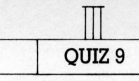

QUIZ 9

ANSWERS ON PAGE 83

A Alan Oakman, the Warwickshire coach, unexpectedly found himself umpiring in the Edgbaston Test of 1973, England vs West Indies. Who should have been officiating?

B Where is the Test ground known as the Gaddafi Stadium?

C Which book has published the detailed scores of all county championship matches since 1864?

D Which famous fast bowler is nicknamed 'Paddles'?

E Which West Indian batsman trod on his stumps while hooking Dennis Lillee for six in the 1975 World Cup final?

F Which wicketkeeper claimed most victims in English first-class matches in 1987?

G Which country without its own first-class team stages official one-day internationals?

H Which captain in a Benson & Hedges match declared the innings closed at 0 for 0?

I What was the result of the ten-day Test match between England and South Africa in 1938–39?

J To whom did John Lever concede 5 runs at Chelmsford in 1986?

QUIZ 10

ANSWERS ON PAGE 84

A Which Pakistan Test bowler has only two fingers on his right hand?

B How were England humiliated at Christchurch in 1983–84?

C Which recent Yorkshire and England fast bowler played soccer for Manchester United and Huddersfield Town?

D Which two bowlers dismissed Surrey for 14 in 1983?

E Rob Bailey and Graeme Hick shared what batting record in 1986?

F Who was the principal wicketkeeper on the England B tour to Sri Lanka in 1986?

G Who caught Derek Randall off the final ball in the 1985 NatWest final to give Essex victory by one run?

H On which ground did Mike Gatting lead England in a Test for the first time?

I Which Indian batsman played for England on the 'Bodyline' tour?

J Which Welshman had his England cap controvertially removed?

QUIZ 11

ANSWERS ON PAGE 84

A What, in Test terms, do Graham Gooch and Neil Fairbrother have in common?

B Which ground apart from Lord's did Middlesex use for home matches in 1987?

C Which county was robbed of the Championship title by rain in 1974?

D Which bowler captured Gatting's wicket in the 1987–88 World Cup, when the England captain tried the reverse sweep?

E Who scored the slowest hundred in Test cricket?

F What fielding record did Micky Stewart achieve in 1957?

G The first World Cup hat-trick was achieved in 1987–88 by which bowler?

H Which Australian captain was reduced to tears in 1984–85 at Brisbane?

I When was the last time Test matches in England were arranged for four days?

J What did Chris Lethbridge achieve with his first delivery in a first-class match?

QUIZ 12

ANSWERS ON PAGE 85

A Who replaced Graham Dilley when he withdrew from the fourteen-man England squad for the 1987–88 World Cup?

B Which of these three grounds have staged one-day internationals, Taunton, Scarborough and Chelmsford?

C Which player in English first-class cricket is nicknamed 'The Gnome'?

D Who said, 'I try to hit a batsman in the rib cage and I want it to hurt so much that the batsman doesn't want to face me any more'?

E Which Indian emulated Gary Sobers's feat of 6 sixes in one over?

F Which West Indian spectacularly ran out Graham Gooch in the 1987 Lord's Bicentenary match?

G Who was the only Englishman to score a hundred in the 1987–88 World Cup?

H For which two English counties has the Indian captain, Kapil Dev, appeared?

I Which brotherhood launched Worcestershire into first-class cricket?

J Which Essex cricketer used a bicycle to move from fine leg to third man in a county match?

QUIZ 13

ANSWERS ON PAGE 85

A   Whose only Test appearance so far was on his home ground at Edgbaston in 1984?

B   How many Lord's cricket grounds have there been?

C   Which former Derbyshire batsman is now a well-known TV playwright?

D   Which Indian spinner appeared for Derbyshire from 1973 to 1975?

E   True or False? Ian Botham failed to score a century when he captained England.

F   Who was adjudged the Fielder of the Match in the 1987 Lord's Bicentenary game?

G   Which Indian batsman scored an unbeaten 36, while surviving the full 60 overs in a 1975 World Cup game?

H   Which Test captain wrote: *Lambs to the Slaughter*?

I   Which famous fast scorer of the Edwardian era was known as 'The Croucher'?

J   Which ex-England fast bowler became 'Pipeman of the Year'?

QUIZ 14

ANSWERS ON PAGE 86

A Against whom did Sri Lanka gain their first Test victory?

B A feature of which ground is called 'The Hill'?

C Who holds the record for the most centuries in an English season?

D Which Essex spinner did Glamorgan bring back to first-class cricket in 1979?

E Which England batsman was given out 'obstructing field' in 1951?

F Which former Yorks and Worcestershire wicketkeeper died while officiating as umpire in a first-class match in 1970?

G What is the record number of sixes hit in a John Player Sunday League innings?

H Which former Australian captain is reported to have lost £100,000 when his accountant disappeared in December 1985?

I To which country did England first send a touring team?

J Which Pakistani Test cricketer claimed he was used as a drug-runner, the drugs being hidden in his batting gloves, during the 1986–87 tour to Australia?

QUIZ 15

ANSWERS ON PAGE 86

A In 1976 a player became the oldest cricketer to represent England in the post-war era. Name him.

B What is the name of the ground used for Test cricket in Wellington, New Zealand?

C Which county won the Championship seven times in succession in the 1950s?

D Which Australian fast bowler signed for Middlesex in 1981, but scarcely played?

E Which New South Wales twins both scored hundreds in the same first-class innings in 1987–88?

F Who dropped three vital catches off deliveries hit by Hadlee in the 1987 NatWest final?

G In what year did the first one-day international take place?

H Whom did the New Zealand selectors choose to replace Jeff Crowe in the Third Test vs England in 1987–88?

I What game other than cricket is regularly played at Lord's?

J Which cricket rebel had poetic licence?

QUIZ 16

ANSWERS ON PAGE 86

A Who was dropped from the 1958–59 MCC team to Australia because of articles written by him in the *Daily Mail*?

B Which two counties have used Abbeydale Park for their home matches since the war?

C How long is the lunch interval in a County Championship match?

D Which Australian fast bowler's Test career came to an abrupt end due to his 'throwing' action in the 1950s?

E Who holds the record individual score in a first-class match?

F Which Australian batsman, when selected as twelfth man, came on the field dressed as a waiter in a Test match?

G What fate befell Yorkshire in 1973 and Derbyshire in 1985 in the Gillette/NatWest Trophy?

H Which Surrey player transformed Northants in 1949?

I Where did London County stage first-class matches and who captained their side?

J To which cricketing family do Brian, Eric, Geoff and Bill belong?

QUIZ 17

ANSWERS ON PAGE 87

A   Which pair of brothers played for England in 1957?

B   Where is the Sabina Park ground situated?

C   Who, in 1985, played in first-class cricket for both Surrey and Essex?

D   The wife of which left-arm bowler wrote more than one book on cricket in the 1980s?

E   Eighty by Ian Botham gave that great all-rounder yet another record in English cricket. What record?

F   Who left Kent after the 1979 season in order to further his career behind the wicket?

G   In the Gillette/NatWest competition only once have both sides scored the same number of runs in the final. When and who?

H   Has Geoff Boycott captained England in England?

I   Who took 300 wickets in an English first-class season?

J   For which county since 1945 have three Whites, a Black and a Gray played?

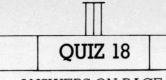

QUIZ 18

ANSWERS ON PAGE 88

A Which two countries compete for the Frank Worrell Trophy?

B On which ground in England has play taken place in a Test on a Sunday?

C England, Scotland and Ireland have all raised first-class teams, has Wales taken part in first-class matches?

D When Laker took nineteen wickets in a Test, who took the remaining one?

E Name the three 'W's.

F If the fieldsman is standing on the boundary line when he catches the ball, does the umpire signal six, or does he give the batsman out?

G Which batsman has scored most runs in one-day internationals?

H Who captained Hampshire to their first Championship title in 1961?

I Who originally set off from England in search of 'The Ashes'?

J Which two post-war England footballers, also won Test caps?

QUIZ 19

ANSWERS ON PAGE 88

A Which two sides played Test cricket against England in England in 1986?

B After Lord's, which is the oldest cricket ground in England that currently stages Test matches?

C Name the unfortunate bowler off whom Gary Sobers hit 6 sixes in 1968?

D Which England fast bowler of the 'Bodyline' series, captained his country fifteen years later?

E Who partnered Peter May in a record fourth wicket stand of 411 for England vs West Indies?

F Who did David Ripley succeed as Northants wicketkeeper?

G When was the first World Cup staged?

H Which cricketer's father captained the 1949 touring team to England?

I What was unique about the County Championship of 1919?

J Name the Labour MP who played for Glamorgan – he was Attorney-General from 1974 to 1979?

QUIZ 20

ANSWERS ON PAGE 88

A Which notable Australian fast bowler declined Packer's offer to join his 'Circus'?

B Which groundsman published his autobiography in the 1980s?

C Which county has a fox on its badge?

D Who took four wickets in four balls in a 1972 Championship match?

E For which county did Walter Keeton and Charlie Harris open the batting?

F Which South African in 1965 was a 'Cricketer of the Year' on account of his fielding ability?

G Who are the only side to lose to Combined Universities since 1980 in the Benson & Hedges Cup?

H Which Pakistani Test cricketer captained Kent in the 1970s?

I The first Test match in England was played at Lord's. True of false?

J Which West Indian Test cricketer threw his bat through an Old Trafford dressing room window?

QUIZ 21

ANSWERS ON PAGE 89

A   Who is Sunil Gavaskar's Test-playing brother-in-law?

B   Which first-class county plays matches at Milton Keynes?

C   Who hit a hundred in his first Championship match and took a wicket with the first ball he bowled in the Championship?

D   Which unorthodox spinner baffled England in 1950–51 – his only Test series?

E   Who scored the most first-class hundreds in the 1987 English season?

F   How many runs are scored if the fielder stops the ball with his cap?

G   Which non-Test playing countries took part in the 1975 World Cup?

H   Who in the 1980s captained both Worcestershire and Warwickshire?

I   A.P.F. Chapman captained England to victory in the Fifth Test of 1926 after four draws. Who led England in the drawn games?

J   What was brave about Rick McCosker's innings in the 1977 Centenary Test?

QUIZ 22

ANSWERS ON PAGE 90

A Prior to Chris Broad and Tim Robinson opening for England, when was the last time two players of the same county performed this task?

B To which ground did first-class cricket return in 1987 after a gap of more than ten years?

C When was the last time two counties shared the Championship title?

D Which fast bowler played for four first-class counties, starting with Sussex and ending with Glamorgan?

E Who hit the fastest 50 in first-class cricket?

F Which substitute was allowed to bowl in a first-class Championship match in the 1980s?

G When was the Sunday League instituted in England?

H Who led South Africa on their last Test tour to England?

I When did New Zealand make their first tour to England?

J South America toured England playing three-day first-class matches. True or false?

QUIZ 23

ANSWERS ON PAGE 90

A   India's innings of 97 all out against West Indies in Kingston in 1975–76 contained only five wickets credited to the bowlers. Why?

B   Why do Worcestershire no longer stage matches at Dudley?

C   What birds feature on the Sussex County Cricket Club badge?

D   Which bowler was playing for England on the same day as his brother was representing England on the rugby field?

E   Who scored a hundred on his first-class début in a 1986 County Championship match?

F   Which Yorkshire wicketkeeper was allowed to sit his A level exam at 6.00 a.m. so that he could finish in time to play for his county?

G   Which country qualified with Sri Lanka for the 1979 World Cup, due to success in the ICC Trophy?

H   Derbyshire had no less than five official captains in the 1970s – Buxton, Bolus, Taylor, Barlow and who else?

I   Which of these three counties have not taken part in the Minor Counties competition: Denbighshire, Westmoreland, Monmouth?

J   Whose biography by Simon Barnes is entitled *A Singular Man*?

QUIZ 24

ANSWERS ON PAGE 91

A Who has hit two double centuries for Pakistan against England?

B Can a match be played using more than one pitch?

C Between 1864 and 1987 all but three present-day first-class counties have won a Championship title. Name the three.

D Which bowler in 1963 became the youngest to take 100 first-class wickets in his début season?

E Who is the only batsman to score two double centuries in the same match?

F Which 1988 England selector was regarded as one of the finest slip fielders of his day?

G For which county, other than Yorkshire, did Fred Trueman play one-day cricket?

H Which Australian state did Tony Lock lead to a Sheffield Shield title?

I Who captained Australia during the 'Bodyline' tour?

J Two cricketing brothers found new first-class counties in 1987, one at the start of the year, the other at the end. Name them.

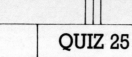

QUIZ 25

ANSWERS ON PAGE 91

A Which county had four players in the England vs New Zealand match at Wellington in 1987–88?

B In which city is Eden Gardens situated?

C For whom did Javed Miandad and Younis Ahmed create a fourth wicket record partnership?

D Which Surrey bowler took four wickets in five balls in 1985?

E Which English batsman made his Test début in the Lord's match of 1980 vs Australia?

F Who was the principal wicketkeeper in the Australian side which toured England in 1985?

G When was the Benson & Hedges Tournament first staged in England?

H Who succeeded Boycott as captain of Yorkshire in 1979?

I Which British Prime Minister played first-class cricket in his younger days?

J Whose benefit yielded a record amount in 1980?

QUIZ 26

ANSWERS ON PAGE 91

A Which all-rounder was the first to score a century and take ten wickets in a match in Tests?

B How many grounds have staged first-class cricket on the Isle of Wight since 1945?

C For which first-class counties did the brothers, Mushtaq and Sadiq Mohammad play?

D Who asked his brother to bowl under-arm and his action resulted in a change in the regulations?

E Which two South African brothers played for the same county in 1987?

F Why was Dickie Bird sitting on the wicket during the Test match at Lord's in 1973?

G Which county lost in the final of both one-day knock-out competitions in 1987?

H Who is the only English captain since the war to lead his country on two Test tours of Australia?

I Known as 'The Nonpareil Bowler', which early cricketer was 35-years-old before he played his first match at Lord's and was still bowling splendidly when nearly 60?

J Who played for India in 1946 under one name and against India in 1952–53 under another?

QUIZ 27

ANSWERS ON PAGE 92

A In the four series between 1976 and 1984 involving England and West Indies, West Indies won eleven matches. How many did England win?

B How many grounds have been used for Test cricket in Bombay?

C Who scored four successive hundreds in English first-class cricket in 1977?

D Which two Australian bowlers were the mainstay of the Leicester attack in the 1940s?

E Which Middlesex batsman in 1986 completed his feat of scoring centuries against all the other sixteen first-class counties?

F Which West Indian Test wicketkeeper gained a blue at Cambridge in 1952?

G The side batting first has won all four World Cups. True or False?

H Who led Yorkshire to four post-war Championship titles?

I Which two first-class touring teams visited England in 1954?

J What did Jeremy Coney and Dickie Bird have in common in 1986?

QUIZ 28

ANSWERS ON PAGE 92

A   Who batted 95 minutes for England against Australia before scoring his first run?

B   Who made the famous hit over the pavilion at Lord's?

C   If two counties finish level on points at the head of the Championship table, which additional factor is used to decide the title?

D   Who took 10 for 10 in a first-class innings?

E   How many ways can a batsman be given out?

F   Which Australian Test wicketkeeper played for Buckinghamshire from 1951 to 1964?

G   What record did Alvin Kallicharran create in the NatWest Trophy in 1984?

H   Who left Yorkshire to captain Leicestershire in 1969?

I   Who were known as the 'Middlesex Twins'?

J   Which tiny Lancashire batsman described his bowling as 'Flighted filth'?

QUIZ 29

ANSWERS ON PAGE 93

A Which bowler bowled most balls in a single Test match?

B Which first-class side use Fenner's as their home ground?

C What is the maximum number of points a county can obtain from a single Championship match in 1988?

D Which controversial bowler performed the hat-trick in the Lord's Test of 1960?

E Which two England batsmen both hit double centuries in the Madras Test of 1984–85?

F Which Kent wicketkeeper in 1962 was put in as nightwatchman and then hit 121 before lunch the next morning?

G Which West Indian pace bowler created a new best-bowling record in the Benson & Hedges Cup in 1978?

H Which BBC TV commentator captained Australia in the 1960s?

I Which former England captain was editor of *The Cricketer* magazine for more than thirty years?

J Which Somerset cricketer was known as 'Robinson Crusoe'?

QUIZ 30

ANSWERS ON PAGE 93

A Name the umpire who featured in the row with Mike Gatting in Pakistan in 1987–88?

B What is the maximum length of time the pitch can be rolled before the start of an innings?

C Which county badge features three pears?

D Which Gloucestershire player twice performed the feat of a hundred and a hat-trick in the same match in the 1970s?

E Who equalled Jessop's record of hitting 200 in two hours in 1976?

F Who is the only fieldsman to hold 1,000 catches in his first-class career?

G Who took a hat-trick in the Benson & Hedges final of 1974 for Leicestershire vs Surrey?

H Who led the Rest of the World vs England in the five-match series of 1970?

I Which county joined the Championship in 1905?

J Both the first ever Test match and the 1977 Centenary Test ended with the same result. What was it?

QUIZ 31

ANSWERS ON PAGE 94

A The selection of which cricketer caused the cancellation of MCC's 1966–67 tour?

B Who plays at The Saffrons?

C Which leg-break bowler moved from Middlesex to Notts in 1974?

D Who has taken a hat-trick most times in first-class cricket?

E Who was dropped from the England side in 1965 after scoring 137 in seven and a quarter hours?

F Which Australian wicketkeeper captained his country in 1968?

G When Zimbabwe played Young Australia in a series of five one-day internationals in 1985, what was the rather surprising result?

H Who captained South Africa in their 'Tests' against the Australians in 1985–86?

I In what year was the *Playfair Cricket Annual* first issued?

J Who are the Goose and the Big Bird?

QUIZ 32

ANSWERS ON PAGE 94

A   Who had a batting average of 99.94 in his Test career?

B   What is the name of the Test ground in Madras?

C   Who is the cricket manager of Nottinghamshire?

D   Which English bowler of the present day holds the record bowling analysis in an innings in the West Indies?

E   What is the highest partnership in English first-class cricket?

F   Which wicketkeeper became the Surrey coach when he retired from county cricket in 1958?

G   How many Minor Counties take part in the 1988 NatWest Trophy competition?

H   Which England captain wrote *Test Kill*?

I   Which cricket journalist was also music critic of *The Manchester Guardian*?

J   Who was the 'Brylcreem Boy'?

QUIZ 33

ANSWERS ON PAGE 95

A   Which country won the 1987–88 series between England and New Zealand?

B   Who was the TCCB Inspector of Pitches in 1987?

C   Yorkshire have won most Championship titles since 1864, which county is second in the list?

D   Which bowler was vice-captain of the West Indian team to India in 1987–88?

E   Which batsman has scored the most runs in his first-class career?

F   What is the maximum permitted width of a cricket bat?

G   Which insurance company sponsored the World Cup Competitions of 1975, 1979 and 1983?

H   When Ian Botham captained England, who was his county captain?

I   On what ground was George Parr's tree situated?

J   How did the weather affect events at Lord's on 27 March 1987?

QUIZ 34

ANSWERS ON PAGE 95

A Who made his début in Test cricket for Australia in 1986–87 having played in only six first-class matches?

B On which ground did Gary Sobers score the Test-record 365 runs?

C What record connects Steve O'Shaughnessy and Percy Fender?

D Who was the last bowler to capture 200 first-class wickets in an English season?

E Which Australian batsman was given out 'handled ball' in the Perth Test of 1978 vs Pakistan?

F Which county play cricket on the Aigburth Ground?

G What is the minimum number of overs allowed to produce a definite result in a Sunday League game?

H When did Tony Lewis, the former Glamorgan cricketer and BBC commentator, captain England?

I Who is generally regarded as the perfector of 'googly' bowling?

J What cricketing post has the Duke of Edinburgh been appointed twice – the only person in the twentieth century to be so honoured?

QUIZ 35

ANSWERS ON PAGE 95

A When was the first time 'twin Test tours' were introduced into England?

B Where apart from Trent Bridge did Notts play a home match in 1987?

C What did Ian Folley, Mike Watkinson and Pat Patterson all achieve in 1987?

D Which famous pair of fast bowlers had Russell and Ross as their second Christian names?

E Which batsman missed a Championship season when he moved from Gloucestershire to Worcestershire in the 1960s?

F What is the umpiring signal for a no ball?

G Which county has won the Sunday League most times?

H Which Hampshire captain and England batsman wrote *Sticky Wickets*?

I For whom did Julius Caesar play cricket?

J Who won the Silk Cut Challenge for all-rounders in 1984, 1985 and 1987?

QUIZ 36

ANSWERS ON PAGE 96

A   Which Australian scored a century on his first-class début and a century on his Test début?

B   Name the Test match ground at Brisbane?

C   Who was the son of a former England captain, who gained his Middlesex county cap in 1987?

D   Which England bowler missed the whole of the 1987 season due to back trouble – Kent is his county?

E   For which county did England batsman Walter Hammond play?

F   What is the height (above ground) of the wicket?

G   Who won the man of the match award in the 1987 NatWest final?

H   Which England captain drowned in a shipping accident in 1930?

I   Which Australian opening batsman wrote *Brightly Fades The Don*?

J   What is the highest individual score ever made in any class of cricket?

QUIZ 37

ANSWERS ON PAGE 96

A Who scored most runs for England in the 1987 Test series in England vs Pakistan?

B Which of the six current English Test grounds is the youngest in terms of Test matches played there?

C He began his county championship career at the age of thirty-eight and hit 3,000 runs in 1961 English season. Who was he?

D Apart from Taunton, Somerset staged home Championship matches on two other grounds in 1987. Which were they?

E At Leeds in 1955, he batted two hours for England making only eight runs and was nicknamed the 'Barnacle'. Who was he?

F Who was the Middlesex wicketkeeper in the 1950s who also played soccer for England?

G How many times has the World Cup competition been staged?

H Captain of two counties, he managed Lancashire from 1982 to 1986. Name him?

I Who was the nephew of Ranjitsinhji, who also played for Sussex and England?

J Which umpire wrote the *Umpire's Lament*, and had an aversion to dogs?

QUIZ 38

ANSWERS ON PAGE 97

A Who scored the first ever Test match hundred?

B Kennington Oval is the home of Surrey CCC, but who plays in Kensington Oval?

C Who is the youngest player to achieve the 'double' of 1,000 runs and 1,000 wickets in an English season? He performed the feat in 1949.

D Who has taken most wickets in an England vs Australia Test series?

E Who was the last batsman to complete 1,000 first-class runs before the end of May?

F Which county wicketkeeper caught eight batsmen in an innings in 1985?

G Name the first player to reach the 1,000 runs and 100 wickets double in Sunday League matches.

H Who was the bespectacled all-rounder from South Africa who captained Derbyshire in the 1970s?

I Known as 'The Guv'nor' he played for Surrey in over 500 matches as a batsman?

J What mode of dismissal has never occurred in England first-class cricket?

QUIZ 39

ANSWERS ON PAGE 97

A Which son of an England cricketer made his England début in 1984–85?

B How many times has a Test match in England been a total wash out and at what venue(s)?

C Who was the left-arm spinner who topped the Glamorgan bowling averages in his début season of 1976, but then decided to retire?

D Which spinner was recalled to the New Zealand side for the Wellington Test of 1987–88? He toured England first in 1978?

E Which Warwickshire batsman's Test career ended abruptly when he signed for Packer's Circus?

F Do the current Laws of Cricket allow eight balls per over?

G In English county limited-overs cricket, when can a captain declare his innings closed?

H Who captained New Zealand on their 1978 tour to England? It was his third English tour.

I Created a life peer in 1969, he was West Indies' outstanding all-rounder in the inter-war period. Who was he?

J Who was the English selectors unusual choice during the 1956 home series versus Australia?

QUIZ 40

ANSWERS ON PAGE 98

A Chairman of the English selectors from 1969 to 1981, he played fifty-one Tests for his country. Who was he?

B Which is the only Australian Test ground capable of accommodating 100,000 spectators?

C Which team hit a record 721 in a single day's play against Essex?

D Who has captured 100 first-class wickets in a season most times since 1969?

E Who, with the Christian names Charles William Jeffrey, moved counties in the 1980s to further his career?

F Which England wicketkeeper is now the NCA Director of Coaching?

G What is the maximum number of overs a bowler can deliver in the NatWest Trophy?

H Who captained Notts before Clive Rice?

I Known as the 'Big Ship' he weighed twenty stone and led Australia to victory in 1921. Who was he?

J He played for the West Indies in England in 1939, then after the war for Northants and Essex. Who is he?

QUIZ 41

ANSWERS ON PAGE 98

A   In 1979 he emulated his father by being chosen to go to England with the Indian Test side, unlike Dad he was not sent home half way through the programme. Who was he?

B   Which county headquarters also houses a team in the Football League?

C   Who is the only cricketer to appear in first-class cricket in England both before the First World War and after the Second World War?

D   A qualified teacher, born in Cheshire, he made his England début in 1981. Who is this fast bowler?

E   Which number eleven batsman obtained a seasonal first-class average of 102.00 in 1953?

F   In a twelve-a-side match, how many players are allowed to field according to the current laws?

G   Which country found themselves unexpectedly competing in the 1979 ICC Trophy?

H   Greg Chappell captained Australia in four of the five series versus England between 1976–77 and 1980. Who led Australia in the other series (1978–79)?

I   What unique feature is connected with the Test career of Ken Cranston?

J   Known as 'Tom' he was christened Horace Edgar and captained Warwickshire in the 1950s. Who was he?

47

QUIZ 42

ANSWERS ON PAGE 99

A   What is the record tenth wicket partnership for Test cricket?

B   In which city is the Newlands Cricket Ground situated?

C   Who is the present Northants Secretary, formerly of Yorkshire and Cambridge University?

D   Twice suspended by the TCCB in the 1970s due to his suspect bowling action, he ended his county cricket career with Lincolnshire. Who was he?

E   Who is the only cricketer to hit two scores above 400 in first-class matches?

F   Is the ball regarded as 'dead' if it strikes an umpire?

G   Who created a bowling record in the Gillette Cup Competition when he took 7 for 15 for Kent in 1967?

H   Who captained the West Indian rebel side to South Africa in 1983–84?

I   What is the highest individual Test score made in England?

J   When did India last play South Africa in a Test match?

QUIZ 43

ANSWERS ON PAGE 99

A Who was the first player to hit a century and double century in the same Test match?

B Which county has its headquarters at a former racecourse?

C Who was the post-war spinner for Gloucestershire and England, christened Cecil, but more usually known as Sam?

D How did the term 'hat-trick' originate?

E Which famous batsman holds the record for the fastest triple century?

F In a match lasting more than one day, do the laws permit the outfield to be mown after the first morning?

G Which bowling wicketkeeper led Warwickshire to victory in the Gillette Cup in his first year as captain?

H Who emulated his father by captaining England in Tests against South Africa in 1948–49?

I Who, in cricketing terms, is Pudsey's greatest son?

J Who was the last Church of England clergyman to play for England?

QUIZ 44

ANSWERS ON PAGE 100

A Which Derbyshire fast bowler made only two Test appearances, once in 1949 and once in 1961?

B Which English county ground is within sight of a cathedral across a river?

C Who sprang to instant fame when he dismissed Don Bradman twice at Old Trafford in 1948?

D Which Leicestershire player noted for his 'donkey drops' played once for England in 1953–54, when he was acting as manager of the touring side?

E Which burly batsman lost the sight of his left eye in a road accident in 1969?

F How often in a match should the umpires change ends?

G Who scored a century in the first match of the 1987–88 World Cup – he was playing for Pakistan at Hyderabad?

H Which well-known captain called his autobiography *I Don't Bruise Easily*?

I Which England and Worcestershire batsman retired from county cricket at the age of thirty-two to become national coach in New Zealand?

J Who was known as 'Noddy' and scored more than 20,000 first-class runs, playing for Lancashire and England in the 1950s and 1960s?

QUIZ 45

ANSWERS ON PAGE 100

A Which Essex and England batsman was Chairman of the TCCB when the Packer row burst in 1977?

B Which Test ground has been used to stage the FA Cup final?

C Who won the County Championship in 1981, having not won the title since 1929?

D Which slow left-armer moved from Leicestershire to Northants in 1986?

E What was unusual about Rameez Raja's dismissal in the one-day international between England and Pakistan in 1987–88?

F How many runs behind on first innings do the side batting second have to be for the follow on to be enforced in a three-day match?

G Who made the highest individual score for Australia in the final of the 1987–88 World Cup?

H Which former England captain wrote *Double Century* in 1987?

I What is the name of India's equivalent of the County Championship?

J Which cricketer did MCC have to persuade the Government to release from the mines in order that he could represent England?

QUIZ 46

ANSWERS ON PAGE 101

A What was the unfortunate end to Ewan Chatfield's innings in the England versus New Zealand Test at Auckland in 1975?

B Where, according to Neville Cardus, was it 'always afternoon and 304 for 2'?

C Apart from cricket, at which other sport has David Acfield of Essex found fame?

D What outstanding bowling feat do Australian Massie and Indian Hirwani have in common?

E By coincidence, the same batsman was at the crease when both John Edrich and later Geoff Boycott reached their hundredth hundred. Who was he?

F When was the present Code of Laws first published?

G Which Pakistani cricketer, other than Imran Khan, has scored 1,000 runs and taken 50 wickets in one-day internationals?

H Name the England captain forced through injury to return home in the middle of the 1983–84 tour of Pakistan?

I Who wrote *The Cricket Field*, the first standard history of the game, which ran through nine editions from 1851 to 1887?

J What did Chris Balderstone do on 15 September 1975, which in sporting terms was a kind of 'double'?

QUIZ 47

ANSWERS ON PAGE 101

A Against which country did Sunil Gavaskar make most of his Test hundreds?

B Name the cricket ground used for Test matches since 1930 in Christchurch, New Zealand?

C Only one English batsman has scored a triple century while touring in Australia. He performed this feat in 1962–63. Who was he?

D Who was the first bowler to take 300 Test wickets?

E Who made the highest individual score in first-class cricket in England in 1987?

F Who was the last wicketkeeper to achieve 100 dismissals in a season? He accomplished the feat in 1964.

G Who recorded a century partnership for the last wicket in a one-day international in 1984 at Old Trafford?

H Who captained Glamorgan in 1985?

I When did county cricket change from five balls per over to six?

J Who wrote *Spin Me a Spinner*, a report of the 1962–63 Test series between England and Australia?

QUIZ 48

ANSWERS ON PAGE 102

A Who was the first West Indian batsman to complete 8,000 Test runs?

B On which ground in 1960 was a County Championship match involving Kent and Worcester completed in a single day?

C What is the lowest total for a side in English first-class cricket?

D Who took all ten wickets in an innings for Sussex at Worthing in 1964?

E In 1970–71, the England Test openers added 100 partnerships for the first wicket in three consecutive innings. Who were the batsmen concerned?

F The number of on-side fieldsmen behind the popping crease is restricted to how many?

G Which county won the Benson & Hedges Cup in 1973, 1976 and 1978?

H Who captained England when they scored the record 903 for 8 declared in 1938?

I In what year did the County Regulations first permit overseas players to appear without residential qualifications?

J Who is the veteran commentator of the BBC 'Test Match Special' team, noted for his schoolboy humour?

QUIZ 49

ANSWERS ON PAGE 102

A   In 1972 who hit a double century in his first Test innings and a century in his second?

B   Where is Essex's county headquarters?

C   Of the sixteen counties that took part in the 1914 Championship, one did not participate in the competition in 1919 – which one?

D   Name the Danish bowler who appears for Derbyshire.

E   Which current Essex batsman scored a century on his début for the county?

F   Which current county wicketkeeper also helped to create the present fourth wicket record partnership in English county cricket?

G   Who, aged 39, was the oldest cricketer to play in the 1983 World Cup?

H   When did Mike Gatting take over as captain of Middlesex?

I   Which famous batsman was knighted in 1953?

J   Name the father and son, both born in South Africa, who have appeared for Worcestershire since the war.

QUIZ 50

ANSWERS ON PAGE 103

A Who is the only player to score a century in each innings of a Test twice in the same series?

B In which city is Edgbaston Cricket Ground?

C In which county was Ian Botham born?

D What is a 'Chinaman'?

E Which batsman was known as the 'Black Bradman'?

F Can a batsman be out off a no ball?

G Name the domestic one-day competition played in India.

H Who was Australia's youngest captain?

I In which year did India first beat England in a Test?

J Which cricketer has the Christian names Wesley Winfield?

QUIZ 51

ANSWERS ON PAGE 103

A Who made South Africa's highest score in Test?

B From 1945 until 1963, the Gentlemen opposed the Players at Lord's and at which other venue?

C Who has made the most consecutive appearances in the County Championship?

D For which country did Lindsay Kline bowl?

E Who, apart from Len Hutton, hit hundreds in England's record score at The Oval in 1938?

F What is the distance between the bowling and popping creases?

G Which counties have yet to win the Gillette/NatWest Competition?

H In which Test series did Mike Smith, Colin Cowdrey and Brian Close share the captaincy of England?

I Which Indian cricketer was known as 'Vinoo'?

J For which county did Paul Downton's father keep wicket?

QUIZ 52

ANSWERS ON PAGE 103

A The principal West Indian batsmen on the 1950 tour to England were Weekes, Worrell and Walcott, but who opened the batting for the team?

B Where is the United Services Ground and which county play there?

C Somerset have never won the County Championship –how many times have the club been runners-up?

D Which Test bowler was nicknamed 'Tufty'?

E For which county other than Hampshire did Barry Richards play?

F Which is the alternative name for silly mid-on?

G When did Sussex win the Sunday League?

H Who was the first Australian to score a hundred in his first Test as captain?

I What is the Duleep Trophy Competition?

J Which Kent cricketer's sister did Graham Dilley marry?

QUIZ 53

ANSWERS ON PAGE 104

A What is the highest total made by Australia in Test cricket?

B Where did Peter Loader perform the first and only post-war Test match hat-trick for England?

C Which batsman has hit most runs in a single day in English first-class cricket?

D Who is the only bowler to take ten wickets in an innings twice in the same season?

E Since the reduction in County Championship cricket in 1969, which batsman has scored most first-class runs in an English season?

F Which wicketkeeper has achieved most dismissals in his first-class career?

G Which company formerly sponsored the Texaco Trophy?

H Which captain led an Australian team to England and returned undefeated in any match?

I The ICC is the world governing body of cricket, what did the initials stand for until 1965?

J For which country has Kevin Curran played cricket?

QUIZ 54

ANSWERS ON PAGE 104

A   Which side won The Ashes in the 1979–80 series?

B   At Edgbaston in the 1985 Test vs Australia, how did Allan Lamb's foot play a vital role in the dismissal of Phillips?

C   Why is the 1988 season a cause for celebration in Glamorgan?

D   Who was Australia's most successful bowler, with eleven wickets, in the 1976–77 Melbourne Centenary Test?

E   Who was the first modern batsman to wear a protective helmet in a Test match?

F   Why was the fire brigade required in the 1959–60 Port of Spain Test?

G   How many overs per side were allowed when the Gillette Cup Competition started?

H   Which spin bowler captained India in England in 1979?

I   Which Test cricketer was reported to have been offered the throne of Albania?

J   What was remarkable about the selection of George Gunn and Wilfred Rhodes for the Test series vs the West Indies in 1929–30?

QUIZ 55

ANSWERS ON PAGE 105

A Where was controversy unexpectedly caused during the 1980 Lord's Test match?

B On what ground did Cliff Gladwin manage to win a Test off the last possible ball in 1948–49?

C What was odd about the County Championship results of both 1949 and 1950? It is most unlikely to happen now.

D Whose nickname was 'Toey'?

E What record did Sunil Gavaskar achieve at Madras in 1983–84?

F Who has taken most catches in Test cricket, excluding wicketkeepers?

G When did Sussex win the NatWest Trophy for the first time?

H Pakistan used two captains in the Test versus Sri Lanka in 1985–86. Who were they?

I What was most unusual about the twenty-three wickets which G.H. Simpson-Hayward took in the 1909–10 series between England and South Africa?

J Which bowler caused a press storm with the use of Vaseline in 1976–77?

QUIZ 56

ANSWERS ON PAGE 105

A How did Botham celebrate India's Golden Jubilee in 1979–80?

B Why were the crowd so happy when Viv Richards and Richie Richardson put on 308 for the third wicket in a Test in the 1983–84 series?

C Which South African fast bowler made his début for Glamorgan in 1987?

D Which Australian bowler created a new record for wickets in a series versus England in 1978–79?

E Whose 'gardening' caused controversy at Johannesburg in 1964–65?

F How did 221 feature in England's favour during the Tests versus Pakistan in 1982?

G What, until 1983, was the unique feature of Greenidge's batting in one-day cricket for Hampshire?

H Colin Cowdrey was appointed captain of the MCC side to the West Indies in 1967–68 owing to an unprecedented move by the selectors. What was it?

I How is Hollywood linked with the first Test between England and South Africa?

J Who retired with 154 not out at St John's in 1982–83 due to his daughter's illness?

QUIZ 57

ANSWERS ON PAGE 106

A Who went home in the middle of the England tour to India in 1981–82 and travelled elsewhere to continue his international cricket?

B What unique record links Madras with Brisbane?

C How did Alan Hill and Martin Jean-Jacques feature in a Derbyshire record in 1986?

D Which bowler headed by a large margin the England Test averages against India in 1984–85?

E Who is the only batsman to score a triple century for Northants?

F Who was the first Australian wicketkeeper to score a century in a Test match?

G What was significant about Viv Richards innings of 189 not out against England in the 1984 one-day international?

H Who captained New Zealand in England in 1986?

I Which team joined the Minor Counties Competition for the first time in 1988?

J Name the wicketkeeper who was flown out to reinforce England in the West Indies in 1959–60?

QUIZ 58

ANSWERS ON PAGE 106

A What tragic event marred the Third Test at Bridgetown in 1980–81?

B Which former Test ground is now in a country that does not play first-class cricket?

C Which 1987 Derbyshire cricketer previously appeared for Lancashire?

D Who was the leading bowler for England in the 1986–87 series versus Australia?

E What two records did Greg Chappell break at Sydney in the Test of 1983–84?

F When fielding for the West Indies in Multan in 1980–81 how did Sylvester Clarke's throwing cause a surprise?

G Who at the start of the 1987 season held all three individual batting records for Worcestershire in one-day competitions?

H Who was appointed captain of Yorkshire for 1987, and whom did he succeed?

I What was the major cricket tournament in India before 1930?

J Who was omitted from the England team after knocking over Sunil Gavaskar at Lord's?

QUIZ 59

ANSWERS ON PAGE 106

A For whom did J.T. Partridge take twenty-five wickets in a Test series in 1964–65?

B Where did oranges feature in a Test during 1984–85 season?

C For which county does the Young England cricketer Mark Alleyne play?

D Who overtook Fred Trueman's Test wicket aggregate in 1975–76, to create a new record for the number of wickets taken in Tests?

E Which Indian wicketkeeper made a century, when going in as nightwatchman versus Australia in 1979–80?

F Which two players shared the wicketkeeping duties for Lancashire in 1987?

G Which bowler holds the record for Leicestershire in both Gillette/NatWest and Sunday League for best bowling in an innings?

H Who resigned as captain of Essex at the end of the 1987 season?

I Who is the only cricketer in a first-class match in England to score a hundred in each innings and take ten wickets?

J Which Sussex bowler was co-opted into the England team in New Zealand in 1983–84 and played his only Test there?

QUIZ 60

ANSWERS ON PAGE 107

A What is the largest victory recorded in Test cricket?

B In which town is the Carisbrook cricket and rugby ground?

C Who took a wicket with his last delivery in the first innings of a match and then a hat-trick with the first three deliveries he bowled in the second innings?

D Who took nine wickets in an innings for Leicestershire in 1985?

E Which player, in a career spanning 1967 to 1982 scored a record number of first-class hundreds for Worcestershire?

F If the batsmen run five and the ball then crosses the boundary, do the five runs count?

G Which English batsman recorded his first one-day international century in the third game of the 1987–88 series against New Zealand?

H Who captained Australia in the first Test against England?

I For which trophy do the Australian states compete in first-class cricket?

J For which batting stroke is Denis Compton best remembered?

QUIZ 61

ANSWERS ON PAGE 107

A Who was the first Pakistan player to score a century on his Test début?

B Which Australian Test ground is in Richmond Park?

C Who were the first sponsors of the English County Championship?

D Which bowler has the forenames Anderson Montgomery Everton?

E Who was the Oxford University freshman, who hit a century on his Test début at Old Trafford in 1959?

F On which ground is the Warner Stand situated?

G Who was the first English batsman to score three hundreds in Prudential one-day internationals in England?

H Did John Edrich ever captain England in a Test match?

I Jim Laker played for two counties, Surrey was one, which was the other?

J What colour caps do West Indian Test players wear?

QUIZ 62

ANSWERS ON PAGE 108

A   Who was the first cricketer to complete the Test double of 2,000 runs and 200 wickets in his career?

B   What is the name of the major cricket ground in Leicester?

C   Name the two brothers both of whom scored 1,000 runs for Sussex in 1987?

D   Warwickshire employed two West Indian born fast bowlers in 1987, one was Gladstone Small, who was the second?

E   Who was the only batsman touring England with Pakistan in 1987 to reach 1,000 first-class runs?

F   Which well-known writer of detective fiction played English first-class cricket?

G   Who, in a one-day international in England, bowled eleven overs conceding only twelve runs in 1980?

H   Who captained England in India in 1981–82?

I   What is the oldest continuous first-class cricket fixture?

J   What have the following in common, M.J.K. Smith, M.P. Donnelly and S.M.J. Woods?

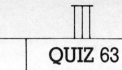

QUIZ 63

ANSWERS ON PAGE 108

A Who did New Zealand beat in their first ever Test victory?

B Melbourne and The Oval were the first and second grounds on which Test cricket was played, which was the third and fourth?

C Who won the first-class counties Second XI competition in 1987?

D Which England fast bowler was injured during the 1970–71 tour to Australia and came home early?

E Which South African batsman hit 26 sixes in his first season with Essex?

F Which wicketkeeper caused a storm of protest when he was injured in the 'Bodyline' series?

G Who led Tasmania to victory in the Austalian one-day competition in 1978–79?

H Who led Sri Lanka for the country's first ever Test?

I Who was the Test umpire, whose career as a first-class cricketer ended when he lost an arm in the First World War?

J In the 1987–88 Under-20s international tournament in Australia, which country took the trophy?

QUIZ 64

ANSWERS ON PAGE 108

A   Who was Geoff Boycott's opening partner in the 1965–66 series against Australia?

B   Which New Zealand ground was first used for Test cricket in 1978–79?

C   Who created a new individual batting record for Somerset in 1985?

D   Which Worcestershire bowler performed two hat-tricks in one match since the Second World War?

E   Which bowler hit Essex's fastest ever hundred in 44 minutes in 1975?

F   Which Derbyshire wicketkeeper took catches off three successive balls in 1958?

G   Which West Indian Test player has hit 6 hundreds in one-day internationals against Australia?

H   Who led England against Bradman's 1948 Australians?

I   When was over-arm bowling first legalized?

J   Which well-known cricket writer's first two forenames are Leslie Thomas?

QUIZ 65
ANSWERS ON PAGE 109

England vs. West Indies – Lord's, 1963: Derek Shackleton is run out by Frank Worrell as Wes Hall appeals. What happened next?

Name the cricket ground and the year this unusual photograph was taken.

C What did both these batsmen do at Taun in a County Championship matc

D Identify this
spin-bowling duo.

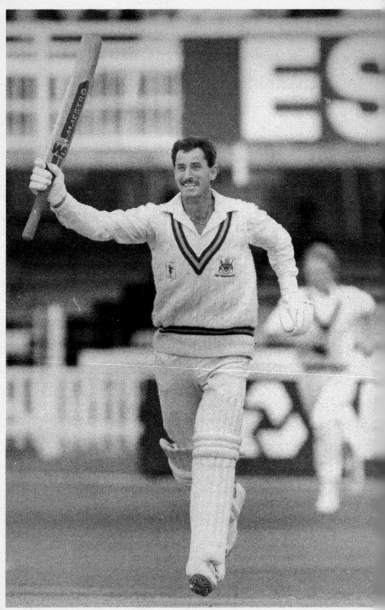

E   Who is this batsman and why is he so happy?

These two slip fielders formed one of cricket's most famous opening partnerships. Who are they?

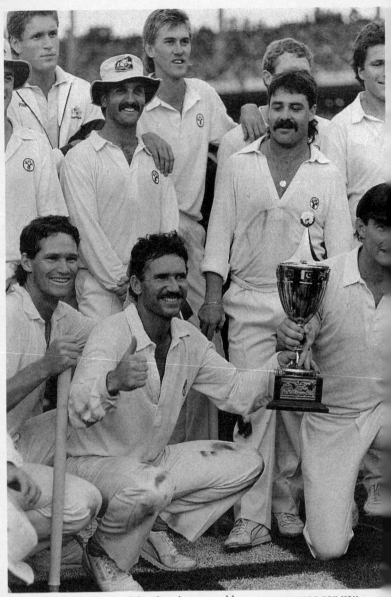

G What is the cause of the thumbs up and how many names can you put to the faces?

Here are two Kent cricketers who captained their county and their country. Who are they, what countries did they lead and what was strange about it?

I   This touring team included King Cole, John Mullagh and Dick-a-Dick. Who are they and what record did they create?

J   Who is getting involved in a spot of bat abuse and when and where did it occur?

ANSWERS

QUIZ 1

A The International Cricket Conference (ICC), which was originally formed in 1909, but has been known by this title only since 1965.

B Bramall Lane, Sheffield, the home of Sheffield United FC. This was once the major Yorkshire cricket ground and a Test was played there in 1902.

C Hampshire. In the late eighteenth century, centred on Hambledon, Hampshire had the strongest county side, but in the nineteenth century cricket in the county was at a low ebb and after years of struggle it was dropped from the ranks of the first-class sides in 1885, though restored in 1895.

D Abdul Qadir of Pakistan. He took 30 wickets at an average of 14.56 in the three-match series, including 9 for 56 in an innings at Lahore.

E Ian Botham, who hit 80 in first-class matches, mainly for Somerset, in 1985.

F Bob Taylor of Derbyshire, who was attending the Lord's Test. He substituted for Bruce French, who had been injured whilst batting.

G Chris Board.

H Len Hutton of Yorkshire. A professional, Hutton was not considered for the county captaincy, as it was traditionally a post for amateurs.

I Gloucestershire from 1870 to 1899, when he resigned over a disagreement.

J Lillee asked for the Queen's autograph.

QUIZ 2

A India, who beat England by two matches to nil with one drawn, and New Zealand who also beat England by winning one match, the other two being drawn.

B The St Lawrence Ground at Canterbury, which is the headquarters of Kent.

C For the first time some Championship matches were allotted four days. Prior to 1988, only Test matches in England have been played over more than three days, though overseas, notably in Australia and India first-class matches have been played over four or more days in the past.

D   Frank Tyson, the Northants and England fast bowler, whose career lasted from 1952 to 1960.

E   Geoff Boycott: 102.53 in 1979 and 100.12 in 1971.

F   Bob Taylor for England vs India at Bombay – all ten were catches.

G   Derbyshire who beat Northants at Lord's in 1981.

H   Ian and Greg Chappell.

I   Hambledon.

J   Being injured they batted one-handed – Marshall at Leeds and Terry at Manchester.

QUIZ 3

A   Dipak Patel, who was born in Nairobi in 1958, came to England in 1967, made his début for Worcestershire in 1976, but has resided in New Zealand since 1980.

B   Headingley, the Test Match Ground in Leeds, headquarters of Yorkshire.

C   Middlesex playing against Worcestershire, just after he had been dropped by the English Test selectors.

D   Fred Titmus in a swimming accident. He recovered and played again for England.

E   Dennis Amiss of Warwickshire.

F   Surrey, for whom Swetman appeared from 1954 to 1961 – he played for England in eleven Tests 1958–59 to 1959–60. His other counties were Notts and Gloucestershire.

G   Lancashire.

H   Alvin Kallicharran, when Clive Lloyd was in dispute owing to Packer's World Series Cricket.

I   Yes, in 1939.

J   Sticky dog is the name given to a type of pitch which helps Underwood's bowling.

QUIZ 4

A   Derek Pringle, the Cambridge University and Essex all-rounder.

B   Cleethorpes, the Lincolnshire seaside resort.

C   Seventeen – the number has remained unchanged since 1921.

D   Peter Loader, who played for Surrey from 1951 to 1963 and for England in thirteen Tests, 1954 to 1958–59.

E   Viv Richards, 322 vs Warwickshire at Taunton

F   Jimmy Binks – 1955 to 1969 was, in fact, the complete span of his first-class career. He played for England, but only in Tests overseas.

G   Ewen Chatfield, the seam bowler, who first played for New Zealand in 1974–75.

H   Nawab of Pataudi led India in England in 1946, though he had previously played for England, his son, also the Nawab, led India in forty Tests, including the 1967 tour to England.

I   West Indies played their first Test in England in 1928, but India did not reach Test status until 1932.

J   Believing that George Davis had been wrongly convicted, some of his friends damaged the pitch at Headingley to draw attention to his case.

QUIZ 5

A   Mike Brearley, Mike Gatting and John Emburey.

B   Sophia Gardens, which has been used by Glamorgan since 1967 – previously the county played adjacent to the Cardiff Arms Park rugby ground.

C   Schweppes sponsored the Championship from 1977 to 1983.

D   Robin Jackman of Surrey. Because he had played for Rhodesia in the previous winter, the Guyana Government refused to allow him in the country, even though he was a member of the England side.

E   Mike Brearley – 312 not out was the only triple hundred of his career.

F   S.C. Griffith, who played in three Tests for England 1947–48 to 1948–49 and appeared for Cambridge University, Surrey and Sussex from 1934 to 1954.

G   At the instant of delivery, four, plus bowler and wicketkeeper.

H   Frank Worrell. He played for West Indies from 1947–48 to 1963 in a total of fifty-one Tests and led West Indies in fifteen, including the 1963 tour to England.

I   Glamorgan joined the Championship in 1921.

J   Mike Denness was born in Lanarkshire and captained England 1973–74 to 1975; Tony Lewis was born in Swansea and captained England in 1972–73 and Tony Greig, born in Queenstown, South Africa, captained England in fourteen Tests ending in 1976–77.

QUIZ 6

A   England and West Indies. The Trophy was introduced by the publishers of the Almanack in 1963, the year of the 100th edition of the annual.

B   This is the name of the ground at Basingstoke used by Hampshire.

C   Scarborough. It was common practice at one time for several seaside resorts to hold 'cricket festivals', notably Hastings, Blackpool, Torquay and Bournemouth, but Scarborough is now the sole survivor of games which are not County Championship matches.

D   Sonny Ramadhin and Alf Valentine came to England in 1950 as two spin bowlers totally unknown to fame and bowled with great success.

E   Sunil Gavaskar played in fifteen first-class matches for Somerset in 1980.

F   Thelston Payne of Barbados, who did not appear in the Test series.

G   Zimbabwe, who qualified by winning the ICC Trophy.

H   Allan Border, the Australian captain.

I   Melbourne in 1877.

J   Raffles, originally in the book *The Amateur Cracksman* by E.W. Hornung, published in 1899 by Methuen.

QUIZ 7

A   Pakistan, whose first Test was in India in 1952–53, when A.H. Kardar led the visiting team.

B   At Brisbane between Australia and West Indies in 1960–61.

C   Test and County Cricket Board (TCCB) held its first meeting in December 1968.

D   Ray Lindwall and Keith Miller. Lindwall took 27 wickets in the Test series and 86 wickets in all first-class matches.

E   P.B.H. May, who led England in forty-one Tests, and also captained Surrey.

F   Arnold Long. He appeared for his native Surrey in 352 matches from 1960 to 1975, and then for Sussex in 97 matches 1976 to 1980.

G   Brian Langford bowled his full quota of eight overs without conceding a run in the match between Somerset and Essex at Yeovil in 1969.

H   Pat Pocock, who made his début for Surrey in 1964 and retired at the end of 1986.

I   Lord Hawke was captain of Yorkshire from 1883 to 1910,

Lord Harris led Kent from 1871 to 1889, but then went to India as Governor of Bombay. His final match for Kent was not until 1911.

J   Dennis Lillee went in to bat carrying a bat made of aluminium.

QUIZ 8

A   At the last moment the South African tour to England was cancelled.

B   Trent Bridge in Nottingham was founded in 1838 by William Clarke.

C   Dusty Hare played ten matches for Notts between 1971 and 1977; Alistair Hignell played appeared for Gloucestershire from 1974 to 1983 in 137 matches.

D   Winston Benjamin from Antigua and George Ferris also from Antigua.

E   Knight first appeared for Surrey in 1968, he then played for Gloucestershire from 1971 to 1975, for Sussex 1976 to 1977 and afterwards returned to Surrey.

F   Keith Miller the Australian fast bowler.

G   The McDonald's Cup has been competed for since 1979–80.

H   Kim Hughes, who played for Western Australia and led Australia in the 1983 World Cup.

I   Herbert Sutcliffe of Yorkshire – Hobbs and Sutcliffe compiled fifteen first-wicket century partnerships.

J   Ganteaume hit 112 on his Test début for West Indies vs England in 1947–48 and Redmond hit 107 for New Zealand vs Pakistan in 1972–73. Neither appeared again in Test cricket.

QUIZ 9

A   Oakman was the coach at Edgbaston and was asked to umpire when Arthur Fagg, on a matter of principle, refused to carry on.

B   The Gaddafi Stadium is in Lahore and has been used for Tests since 1959–60.

C   *Wisden's Cricketers' Almanack* has appeared annually since 1864.

D   Richard Hadlee the New Zealand and Notts bowler, so called on account of his splayed feet.

E   Roy Fredericks.

F   B.J.M. Maher of Derbyshire with 72 catches and 4 stumpings; C.J. Richards of Surrey was second with 74 dismissals.

G   Sharjah.

H   Brian Rose of Somerset. The match was against Worcestershire at Worcester.

I   Known as the 'Timeless Test', the match was supposed to be played until a definite result had been reached, but the England team were forced to leave the match drawn after ten days in order to catch the boat home.

J   Clive Rice. Lever picked up the bat Rice had dropped and fielded the ball with it.

QUIZ 10

A   Azeem Hafeez.

B   Dismissed for less than 100 in both innings – the first time vs New Zealand.

C   Arnie Sidebottom, who played five seasons with Manchester United and two with Huddersfield Town.

D   Norbert Phillip (6 for 4) and Neil Foster (4 for 10) for Essex at Chelmsford.

E   They were the only batsman to hit two double centuries.

F   Steve Rhodes of Worcestershire.

G   Paul Prichard at short mid-wicket.

H   At Headingley in the Second Test vs India.

I   Nawab of Pataudi, who in 1932 was playing for Worcestershire.

J   Alan Jones played for England vs Rest of World in 1970. These matches were billed as 'Test Matches', but the classification was later removed.

QUIZ 11

A   They both failed to score in their first Test innings.

B   Uxbridge.

C   Hampshire.

D   Allan Border the Australian.

E   Mudassar Nazar in 557 minutes for Pakistan vs England at Lahore in 1977–78.

F   Playing for Surrey vs Northants at Northampton, he held seven catches in an innings, the first fieldsman ever to do so in a first-class match.

G   Chetan Sharma dismissed Rutherford, Smith and Chatfield

at Nagpur in the match between India and New Zealand.
H   Kim Hughes after West Indies had defeated Australia by eight wickets.
I   1949 – the four matches against New Zealand were all drawn.
J   He dismissed Geoff Boycott with the first ball he bowled in first-class cricket – for Warwickshire vs Yorkshire in 1981.

QUIZ 12

A   Paul Jarvis of Yorkshire.
B   All three have been used for World Cup matches.
C   Keith Fletcher, the Essex and England batsman.
D   Dennis Lillee, the Australian fast bowler.
E   Ravi Shastri for Bombay against Baroda in the Ranji Trophy in 1984–85.
F   Roger Harper, who also plays for Northants.
G   Graham Gooch with 115 against India in the semi-final.
H   Northants and Worcestershire.
I   The Fosters: B.S., G.N., H.K., M.K., N.J.A., R.E. and W.L. – seven brothers all of whom played first-class cricket for Worcestershire.
J   David East.

QUIZ 13

A   Andy Lloyd, who retired injured having made 10, batting against the West Indies.
B   There have been three in London – the first at Dorset Square used from 1787 to 1810, the second 1811 to 1813 in St John's Wood and the present ground since 1814. *But* there was also a ground called Lord's in Durban, South Africa, used for Test cricket in 1909–10.
C   Peter Gibbs, who played for Derbyshire from 1966 to 1972.
D   Venkataraghavan played 46 matches for Derbyshire.
E   True – Botham never hit a hundred when captaining England.
F   Clive Rice, the captain of Notts and South Africa.
G   Sunil Gavaskar against England – India made 132 for 3.
H   Graham Yallop about the Australia vs England series of 1978–79.
I   Gilbert Jessop the Gloucestershire cricketer.
J   Fred Trueman.

QUIZ 14

A   Against India in Colombo in September 1985 by 149 runs.

B   The Sydney ground in Australia.

C   Denis Compton, who hit 18 in 1947.

D   Robin Hobbs, having played in 325 matches for Essex from 1961 to 1975, appeared for Glamorgan in 1979 as captain.

E   Len Hutton batting against South Africa at The Oval.

F   Syd Buller – he was officiating in the match between Warwickshire and Notts.

G   18 by Derbyshire against Worcestershire at Knypersley in 1985.

H   Ian Chappell.

I   Canada and the United States in 1859.

J   Qasim Omar.

QUIZ 15

A   Brian Close, the former Yorkshire cricketer, then with Somerset, played for England vs West Indies at Old Trafford aged 45 years and 140 days.

B   The Basin Reserve, Wellington has been used for Test since January 1930.

C   Surrey won the Championship from 1952 to 1958 under the captaincy first of Stuart Surridge (1952 to 1956) and then Peter May (1957 and 1958).

D   Jeff Thomson played in only eight matches for Middlesex, due to injury.

E   Steve Waugh and Mark Waugh, born 2 June 1965.

F   Allan Lamb and Robert Bailey.

G   In 1970–71 England vs Australia in Australia.

H   John Wright, the opening batsman, who also plays for Derbyshire.

I   Real tennis.

J   John Snow the England and Sussex fast bowler wrote a book *Cricket Rebel* and also had a book of poems published.

QUIZ 16

A   Johnny Wardle, the Yorkshire left-arm spinner, who wrote articles critical of the Yorkshire Committee.

B   Derbyshire played there in 1946 and Yorkshire have used the ground as their principal Sheffield venue since the closing of Bramall Lane.

C   The lunch interval lasts forty minutes.
D   Ian Meckiff of Victoria.
E   Hanif Mohammad scored 499 for Karachi vs Bahawalpur in Karachi in 1958–59.
F   S.G. Barnes of New South Wales, who had been a regular member of the Australian Test side and was somewhat put out at being chosen only as twelfth man.
G   Both teams were knocked out of the competition by Durham.
H   F.R. Brown, who was appointed captain of Northants that year.
I   London County Cricket Club was a commercial venture and played at Crystal Palace. The managers appointed W.G. Grace as captain.
J   They are the four Edrich brothers who all appeared in first-class cricket, Bill for Middlesex, Brian for Kent and Glamorgan, Geoffrey and Eric for Lancashire.

QUIZ 17

A   Peter and Derek Richardson of Worcestershire, who played in one Test together, vs West Indies at Trent Bridge.
B   In Kingston, Jamaica, it has been used for Test cricket since April 1930.
C   Don Topley, he played for Surrey vs Cambridge University in 1985 and four County Championship matches for Essex.
D   Philippe Edmonds, whose wife Frances wrote *Another Bloody Tour* and *Cricket XXXX Cricket.*
E   Botham hit 80 sixes in first-class matches in 1985.
F   Paul Downton was unable to obtain a permanent place in the Kent side due to the presence of Alan Knott and he therefore decided to move to Middlesex.
G   In 1981 Derbyshire and Northants both scored 235, but the former lost fewer wickets and therefore took the trophy.
H   No, he captained England in four Tests in 1977–78, when the official touring captain, Brearley, went home owing to injury.
I   A.P. 'Tich' Freeman, the Kent spin bowler, took 304 wickets in 1928.
J   Middlesex, namely L.R. White (1946–47), R.A. White (1958–65), R.F. White (1964–66), C.J.R. Black (1970–73) and L.H. Gray (1934–51).

QUIZ 18

A   Australia and West Indies. The trophy was instituted in 1964–65 and named after the West Indian captain.

B   Only one Test match in England has included Sunday play, it was staged at Trent Bridge in 1981.

C   Yes, Wales played first-class matches from 1923 to 1930.

D   Tony Lock, his fellow Surrey spinner.

E   Frank Worrell, Clyde Walcott and Everton Weekes, a famous trio of West Indian batsmen in the 1940s and 1950s.

F   He signals six.

G   Viv Richards of West Indies.

H   Colin Ingleby-MacKenzie, who appeared for Hampshire from 1951 to 1965, being captain from 1958 to 1965.

I   Hon. Ivo Bligh, with a side under his captaincy in 1882–83.

J   Arthur Milton of Arsenal and Gloucestershire and Willie Watson of Yorkshire, Leicestershire and Huddersfield and Sunderland. Milton played outside-right and Watson left-half.

QUIZ 19

A   India and New Zealand.

B   Trent Bridge, Nottingham, which was founded in 1838.

C   Malcolm Nash of Glamorgan.

D   G.O.B. Allen of Middlesex – he led England in the West Indies in 1947–48.

E   Colin Cowdrey of Kent.

F   George Sharp.

G   1975 in England.

H   Walter Hadlee, the captain of the 1949 New Zealanders to England, was the father of Dayle and Richard Hadlee.

I   The matches were restricted to two days each – the experiment was a failure with many games drawn.

J   S.C. Silkin.

QUIZ 20

A   Jeff Thomson.

B   Jim Fairbrother, who was head groundsman at Lord's from 1968 to 1984.

C   Leicestershire.

D   Pat Pocock of Surrey playing against Sussex at Eastbourne

- not only did he take four wickets in four balls, but he went on to take six in nine.
E   Nottinghamshire – they added a century for the first wicket on forty-six occasions, a total only exceeded by two other pairs in the history of the game.
F   Colin Bland. A Rhodesian from Bulawayo, he played twenty-one Tests for South Africa between 1961–62 and 1966–67.
G   Gloucestershire at Bristol by 27 runs in 1984.
H   Asif Iqbal captained Kent in 1977. He also captained Pakistan and played in a total of fifty-eight Tests.
I   False. The first Test in England was arranged by C.W. Alcock, Secretary of Surrey CCC, and played at The Oval in 1880.
J   Viv Richards.

QUIZ 21

A   G.R. Viswanath, who made his début for India in 1969–70 and scored 6,080 runs in Tests, second only to Gavaskar among Indian batsmen.
B   Northants.
C   F.W. Stocks, but not in the same match. He hit 114 for Notts vs Kent in 1946 and later in the same season took a wicket with his first delivery for Notts vs Lancashire. The combined feat is unique in first-class cricket.
D   Jack Iverson of Victoria, whose unorthodox grip of the ball confused England.
E   G.A. Hick of Worcestershire with eight.
F   Five penalty runs are awarded to the batsman.
G   East Africa and Canada. Both played three matches and lost all of them.
H   Norman Gifford captained Worcestershire 1971 to 1980 and Warwickshire 1985 to 1987.
I   A.W. Carr, though he was taken ill during the Fourth Test and for most of the match Jack Hobbs captained the side. There was a great deal of controversy when Chapman replaced Carr for the Fifth Test.
J   He batted with a broken jaw. Bob Willis being the offending bowler.

QUIZ 22

A   In the First Test of 1967, John Edrich and Ken Barrington opened England's second innings. Both batsmen played for Surrey.

B   Kidderminster in Worcestershire.

C   Kent and Middlesex in 1977.

D   Allan Jones played for Sussex 1966 to 1969, Somerset 1970 to 1975, Middlesex 1976 to 1979 and Glamorgan 1980 to 1981. He was the first cricketer to represent four different counties since the qualification rules were introduced in 1873.

E   Clive Inman of Leicestershire hit 50 in eight minutes against Notts at Trent Bridge in 1965.

F   David Brown of Warwickshire substituting for Gladstone Small.

G   The Sunday League in England, sponsored by John Player, was instituted in 1969. It is now sponsored by Refuge Assurance.

H   P.L. van der Merwe led South Africa in 1965 and won the rubber by one match to nil.

I   New Zealand toured England in 1927, but did not play any Tests.

J   True. South America came to England in 1932 and their main matches were accorded first-class status.

QUIZ 23

A   The other five batsman were all absent injured.

B   Mining subsidence has made the wicket unfit for use.

C   Seven martlets.

D   Chris Old; his brother Alan Old was a notable fly-half for England and the British Lions.

E   P.D. Bowler hit 100 not out for Leicestershire vs Hampshire at Leicester.

F   David Bairstow, when making his début in 1970.

G   Zimbabwe.

H   Geoff Miller in 1979.

I   Westmoreland.

J   Philippe Edmonds.

QUIZ 24

A   Zaheer Abbas hit 274 at Edgbaston in 1971 and 240 at The Oval in 1974.

B   Yes, if it becomes unfit for play *and* both captains agree.

C   Sussex, Somerset and Northants. Of these only Somerset have not finished as runners-up.

D   Derek Underwood of Kent, born 8 June 1945.

E   Arthur Fagg of Kent, playing against Essex in 1938.

F   Phil Sharpe of Yorkshire.

G   After leaving Yorkshire, Trueman played for Derbyshire.

H   He played for Western Australia from 1962–63 to 1970–71 – that state won the Sheffield Shield in 1967–68.

I   Bill Woodfull, he also led Australia in England in 1930 and 1934.

J   Alan Butcher moved from Surrey to Glamorgan and his brother Ian from Leicestershire to Gloucestershire.

QUIZ 25

A   Nottinghamshire – Chris Broad, Tim Robinson, Bruce French and Eddie Hemmings.

B   Calcutta – first used for Test cricket in January 1934.

C   The two Pakistani batsmen were playing for Glamorgan against the Australians and put on an unbroken 306 for the fourth wicket in 1985.

D   A.H. Gray for Surrey vs Yorkshire, at Sheffield.

E   Bill Athey, then of Yorkshire, now of Gloucestershire.

F   Wayne Phillips of South Australia – he played in all six Tests.

G   1972.

H   J.H. Hampshire.

I   Sir Alec Douglas-Home played for Middlesex in 1924 and 1925.

J   Jack Simmons of Lancashire received £128,000 in 1980.

QUIZ 26

A   Ian Botham scored 114 and took 13 for 106 for England vsIndia at Bombay in 1979–80.

B   One – at Cowes.

C   Mushtaq played for Northants from 1964 to 1977 and Sadiq for Essex in one match in 1970 and for Gloucestershire from 1972 to 1982.

D   Greg Chappell instructed his brother Trevor to bowl under-arm for Australia in a one-day international to prevent the opposition from scoring.

E   Chris Smith and Robin Smith of Hampshire.

F   There was a bomb scare and the spectators were asked to vacate the stands and go on to the playing area.

G   Northants lost to Yorkshire in the Benson & Hedges and Notts in the NatWest Trophy.

H   J.M. Brearley in 1978–79 and 1979–80.

I   William Lillywhite.

J   A.H. Kardar, who played for India as Abdul Hafeez.

QUIZ 27

A   England failed to win a match.

B   The original Test ground was the Gymkhana Ground in Bombay, but the Cricket Club of India then built the Brabourne Stadium, which was regarded as the most modern venue in India in the 1940s, but owing to an argument over allocation of seating, another stadium was built Wankhede Stadium and this has been used for Tests since 1975.

C   K.S. McEwan, the South African-born Essex batsman.

D   J.E. Walsh and V.E. Jackson, both formerly of New South Wales.

E   C.T. Radley.

F   Gerry Alexander.

G   True. The West Indies won the first two in 1975 and 1979 by 19 and 92 runs; India won by 43 runs in 1983 and Australia by 7 runs in 1987–88.

H   Brian Close captained Yorkshire from 1963 to 1970 – the county won the title in 1963, 1966, 1967 and 1968.

I   Pakistan and Canada.

J   They were both awarded the MBE for services to cricket.

QUIZ 28

A   Godfrey Evans at Adelaide in 1946–47 – he ended with 10 not out in 133 minutes.

B   Albert Trott of Middlesex.

C   Most wins.

D   Hedley Verity for Yorkshire vs Notts in 1932.

E   Ten: bowled, timed out, caught, handled ball, hit the ball

twice, hit wicket, leg before wicket, obstructing the field, run out and stumped.
F Ben Barnett, who played for Australia in England in 1938 and emigrated to London in 1949.
G Kallicharran scored 206 for Warwickshire vs Oxfordshire, the highest individual innings up to that time in the competition.
H Ray Illingworth, who later returned to Yorkshire as manager and captain.
I Denis Compton and Bill Edrich – famous for their batting in 1947.
J Harry Pilling.

QUIZ 29

A Sonny Ramadhin bowled 774 balls in the Edgbaston Test of 1957, playing for West Indies vs England.
B Cambridge University. The ground was opened in 1846 by F.P. Fenner.
C 24 points – 16 for a win plus a maximum of 4 batting and 4 bowling bonus points.
D Geoff Griffin of South Africa who was no-balled for throwing.
E G. Fowler 201, M.W. Gatting 207 – the first time two Englishmen had hit double centuries in the same Test innings.
F Tony Catt playing against Leicestershire at Maidstone.
G Wayne Daniel took 7 for 12 for Middlesex vs Minor Counties (East) at Ipswich.
H Richie Benaud.
Sir Pelham Warner, who played for Middlesex from 1894 to 1920 and played in fifteen Tests, being captain in ten.
R.C. Robertson-Glasgow, who was a noted cricket journalist until his death in 1965.

QUIZ 30

A Shakoor Rana.
B Seven minutes.
C Worcestershire.
D Mike Procter against Essex in 1972 and Leicestershire in 1979.
E Clive Lloyd for West Indies against Glamorgan at Swansea.

F   F.E. Woolley of Kent with 1,018.
G   Ken Higgs for Leicestershire vs Surrey.
H   Gary Sobers of West Indies.
I   Northants became the sixteenth first-class county in 1905.
J   Australia won by 45 runs.

QUIZ 31

A   Basil d'Oliveira, the Worcestershire all-rounder, who was born in South Africa.
B   Sussex, it is the ground used by the county in Eastbourne.
C   Harry Latchman, the Jamaican-born bowler.
D   Doug Wright of Kent (seven times).
E   Ken Barrington, the Surrey batsman.
F   Barry Jarman in the Fourth Test vs England in the absence of Bill Lawry.
G   Zimbabwe won all five matches.
H   Clive Rice, the Transvaal and Notts all-rounder.
I   1948, edited by Peter West.
J   Bob Willis and Joel Garner.

QUIZ 32

A   Don Bradman of Australia – he required four runs in his last Test innings in order to average 100, but was bowled without scoring.
B   Chepauk, home of Madras CC since 1861. The first first-class match was played there in 1915–16 and the first Test in 1933–34.
C   Ken Taylor, the former Warwickshire batsman.
D   Eddie Hemmings, who took all ten wickets in an innings for an International XI vs West Indian XI in 1982–83 in Kingston, Jamaica.
E   555 by H. Sutcliffe and P. Holmes for Yorkshire vs Essex at Leyton in 1932.
F   Arthur McIntyre, who also played for England.
G   Nineteen plus Wales.
H   Ted Dexter – it was a novel.
I   Neville Cardus.
J   Denis Compton, whose portrait was used on hoardings to advertise Brylcreem hair oil.

QUIZ 33

A   All three matches ended as draws.

B   Bernard Flack.

C   Surrey twenty times, two of which were shared.

D   Roger Harper, who also plays for Northants.

E   J.B. Hobbs, who played in 834 matches scoring 61,760 runs at an average of 50.66 He played for Surrey from 1905 to 1934.

F   4¼ inches.

G   Prudential.

H   Ian Botham captained England in England in 1980 vs West Indies and Australia, then in 1980–81 in West Indies and the first two Tests of 1981 in England vs Australia. He captained Somerset in 1984 and 1985, but Somerset's captain from 1978 to 1983 was Brian Rose.

I   Trent Bridge, Nottingham. George Parr was the major batsman of the 1850s.

J   A dinner in a marquee was to be held in Dorset Square, the original site of Lord's Ground, but a gale blew down the marquee.

QUIZ 34

A   Peter Taylor, the New South Wales off-spin bowler.

B   Gary Sobers hit his record at Sabina Park, Kingston, Jamaica, against Pakistan in 1957–58.

C   Both batsmen hit a first-class hundred in 35 minutes: Fender for Surrey vs Northants in 1920; O'Shaughnessy for Lancashire vs Leicestershire in 1983.

D   Tony Lock of Surrey in 1957. He took 212 wickets at an average of 12.02.

E   A.M.J. Hilditch of New South Wales.

F   Lancashire, it is the main ground in Liverpool.

G   20 overs: 10 overs each side.

H   Tony Lewis captained England in eight Tests on the 1972–73 tour of India and Pakistan.

B.J.T. Bosanquet, who played for Middlesex from 1898 to 1919 and in seven Tests for England.

President of the MCC in 1948–49 and 1974–75.

QUIZ 35

A   1965 when South Africa beat England, but England beat New Zealand.

B   Central Avenue, Worksop.
C   They were all capped for Lancashire.
D   Raymond Russell Lindwall and Keith Ross Miller, who made their presence felt most notably in Australia in 1946–47 and in England in 1948.
E   Tom Graveney had to qualify by residence for Worcestershire.
F   Extend one arm horizontally.
G   Kent and Essex have won three titles each: Kent – 1972, 1973 and 1976; Essex – 1981, 1984 and 1985.
H   Lionel, Lord Tennyson, who played for Hampshire from 1913 to 1935 and in nine Tests for England.
I   Surrey from 1849 to 1867 and in one match for Lancashire in 1851, his family which was noted in local cricket came from Godalming.
J   Clive Rice.

QUIZ 36

A   Dirk Wellham, who hit 100 for New South Wales in 1980–81 and 103 for Australia in 1981 in England.
B   The Woolloongabba Ground, usually referred to as the 'Gabba', it has been used for Test cricket since 1931–32.
C   John Carr, whose father Donald Carr captained England in India in 1951–52.
D   Richard Ellison.
E   Gloucestershire from 1920 to 1951 in 405 matches.
F   28 inches.
G   Richard Hadlee of Notts for his 70 not out.
H   J.W.H.T. Douglas drowned in the Baltic in 1930, having played for Essex from 1901 to 1928 and in twenty-three Tests for England.
I   Jack Fingleton, it was his book about the 1948 Australian tour to England.
J   628 not out by A.E.J. Collins in a junior house match at Clifton College near Bristol in 1899.

QUIZ 37

A   Mike Gatting, with 445 runs at an average of 63.57.
B   Edgbaston, Birmingham, which staged its first Test in 1902.
C   Bill Alley of Somerset, born 1919, who made his Somerset début in 1957. He had previously played for New South Wales.

D Bath and Weston-super-Mare.

E Trevor Bailey, the Essex all-rounder, who played for England in sixty-one Tests between 1949 and 1958–59.

F Leslie Compton, the brother of Denis.

G The World Cup in 1987–88 in India and Pakistan was the fourth.

H Jackie Bond, who captained Lancashire for five seasons up to 1972 and then captained Notts in 1974.

I K.S. Duleepsinhji, who played for Sussex from 1924 to 1932 and in twelve Tests for England. At the age of twenty-eight in 1932, ill-health compelled him to retire from first-class cricket.

J Alec Skelding, who played as a fast bowler for Leicester from 1912 to 1929 and was a first-class umpire from 1931 to 1958, retiring aged 72.

QUIZ 38

A Charles Bannerman made 165 retired hurt in the very first Test, batting for Australia vs England.

B Barbados play at the Kensington Oval, which is the Test centre of Bridgetown and staged its first Test in 1929–30.

C Brian Close of Yorkshire, aged 18.

D Jim Laker of Surrey with forty-six in 1956.

E G. A. Hick of Worcestershire in 1988.

F David East of Essex. He caught out the first eight wickets to fall.

G Keith Boyce of Essex, who also played for the West Indies. A serious knee injury prematurely ended his career in 1977.

H Eddie Barlow led Derbyshire from 1976 to 1978. He played thirty Tests for South Africa.

I Bobby Abel, who played for Surrey from 1881 to 1904 and thirteen Tests for England.

J Timed out.

QUIZ 39

A Chris Cowdrey, son of Colin Cowdrey, made his début in India in 1984–85.

B Only two Tests in England have been totally washed out, both arranged against Australia at Old Trafford – in 1893 and 1938.

C   A.W. Allin, who took 44 wickets (average 22.97) in 1976 for Glamorgan, but then decided to give up first-class cricket and return to play for his native Devonshire.

D   Stephen Boock of Otago and Canterbury.

E   Dennis Amiss.

F   Yes. Before a match starts it shall be agreed whether six or eight-ball overs are used.

G   He can't.

H   Mark Burgess the Auckland batsman, who toured England in 1969, 1973 and 1978.

I   Learie Constantine. He toured England with the West Indies teams of 1923, 1928, 1933 and 1939.

J   The selectors actually chose one of themselves, Cyril Washbrook of Lancashire, who returned to Test cricket after an absence of six years and hit 98.

QUIZ 40

A   Alec Bedser of Surrey, the medium pace bowler who was the mainstay of the England attack in the immediate post-war period.

B   Melbourne – the largest official attendance for one day is 90,800.

C   Australian touring team in 1948.

D   Derek Underwood of Kent, his best year being 110 wickets in 1978.

E   Bill Athey moved from Yorkshire to Gloucestershire in 1983–84 and regained his Test place.

F   Keith Andrew, who kept wicket for Northants and England.

G   Twelve overs are allowed per bowler.

H   Mike Smedley.

I   Warwick Armstrong played in fifty Tests for Australia between 1901–02 and 1921.

J   Dr C.B. Clarke played for Northants 1946 to 1949 and for Essex 1959 to 1960. He came from Barbados and represented West Indies in three Tests in 1939.

QUIZ 41

A   Mohinder Amarnath came to England in 1979 and 1984, his father came in 1936 and 1946, but as a disciplinary measure on the 1936 tour sent home just before the First Test.

B Northampton – headquarters of Northants CCC and Northampton Town FC.

C Bill Ashdown of Kent.

D Paul Allott.

E Bill Johnston the left-arm bowler, who scored 102 runs in 17 innings, but was only dismissed once.

F Only eleven are allowed to field according to the current laws.

G Wales came in as a substitute for Gibraltar.

H When Greg Chappell was playing Kerry Packer's World Series Cricket, Graham Yallop led Australia against England in 1978–79.

I Cranston only played two seasons of Championship cricket, both for Lancashire, and played for England in both.

J Tom Dollery the first professional captain of Warwickshire, took the county to the Championship title in 1951.

QUIZ 42

A 151 by B.F. Hastings and R.O. Collinge for New Zealand vs Pakistan at Auckland in 1972–73.

B Cape Town – the ground was opened in 1888 and was used for a Test match in 1888–89.

C Steve Coverdale.

D Geoff Cope the Yorkshire bowler.

E Bill Ponsford the Victoria batsman.

F No.

G Alan Dixon.

H Lawrence Rowe.

I 364 by Len Hutton vs Australia at The Oval in 1938.

J India have never played Test matches against South Africa.

QUIZ 43

A K.D. Walters hit 242 and 103 vs the West Indies at Sydney in 1968–69. Walters was batting for Australia.

B Derbyshire have their County Ground at Derby on the former racecourse.

C Sam Cook, who played in 498 matches for Gloucestershire from 1946 to 1964 and later became a well-known county umpire.

D   Bowlers who performed the hat-trick were given a new hat.
E   Denis Compton hit 300 in 181 minutes for MCC vs North East Transvaal on the 1948–49 MCC tour of South Africa.
F   Yes. The outfield should be mown before play starts each morning.
G   A.C. Smith, who played for Warwickshire from 1958 to 1974.
H   F.G. Mann of Middlesex – F.T. Mann, his father, also played for Middlesex.
I   Len Hutton, the Yorkshire batsman, was born in Pudsey.
J   David Sheppard, who played for Sussex and in twenty-two Tests for England.

QUIZ 44

A   Les Jackson. He played for Derbyshire from 1947 to 1963, generally opening the bowling with Cliff Gladwin, and took 100 wickets in a season ten times.
B   Worcester.
C   Malcolm Hilton the Lancashire spin bowler. He played in four Tests for England in 1950 and 1951–52.
D   Charles Palmer, who began his career with Worcestershire in 1938, moving to Leicestershire in 1950, captaining the latter from 1950 to 1957.
E   Colin Milburn the Northants and England cricketer – he did, in fact, play in some first-class matches after the accident.
F   At the start of each innings.
G   Javed Miandad (103 vs Sri Lanka).
H   Brian Close of Yorkshire and Somerset.
I   Martin Horton.
J   Geoff Pullar.

QUIZ 45

A   Doug Insole, who played for Essex from 1947 to 1963 and in nine Tests for England.
B   The Oval – the FA Cup final was played there from 1871–72 to 1891–92.
C   Nottinghamshire.
D   Nick Cook – he played for Leicestershire from 1978 and gained his first Test cap for England in 1983.
E   Given out obstructing field with his score on 99.

F   150 runs.
G   David Boon scored 75 and received the man of the match award.
H   Tony Lewis, the Glamorgan batsman – the book commemorated two hundred years of cricket at Lord's.
I   The Ranji Trophy (officially the Cricket Championship of India for the Ranji Trophy).
J   Gerry Smithson, the Yorkshire batsman, was selected for the 1947–48 MCC tour to the West Indies, but was conscripted into the mines as a Bevin Boy.

QUIZ 46

A   He was knocked unconscious by a delivery from the England fast bowler Peter Lever, and taken to hospital.
B   Trent Bridge in the 1890s.
C   He was a member of the British Olympic fencing team in 1968 and 1972.
D   Both took sixteen wickets on their Test début.
E   Graham Roope of Surrey and England.
F   1980.
G   Mudassar Nazar.
H   Bob Willis – David Gower took over as captain.
I   James Pycroft.
J   He played for Leicestershire vs Derbyshire at Chesterfield and then in the evening played a League football match for Doncaster Rovers.

QUIZ 47

A   Against the West Indies – he hit 13 hundreds.
B   Lancaster Park, which has been used for Test matches since 1929–30.
C   M.C. Cowdrey scored 307 vs South Australia at Adelaide in 1962–63.
D   Fred Trueman of Yorkshire playing against Australia at The Oval in 1964 took his 300th Test wicket.
E   Javed Miandad, 260 for Pakistan vs England at The Oval.
F   Roy Booth of Worcestershire dismissed 91 batsmen caught and nine stumped.
G   Viv Richards and Michael Holding for the West Indies vs England at Old Trafford.
H   Rodney Ontong.
I   1900.
J   Richie Benaud.

QUIZ 48

A Gary Sobers, whose total was 8,032, average 57.78. He retired in 1973–74.
B Tunbridge Wells on 15 June 1960.
C Twelve by Oxford University vs MCC at Oxford in 1877 and also by Northants vs Gloucestershire at Gloucester in 1907, but in 1810 the 'Bs' were dismissed by England for just 6 runs. At that time a number of the best players in England had a surname beginning with the letter 'B'.
D Ian Thomson.
E Geoff Boycott and Brian Luckhurst.
F Two.
G Kent. They beat Worcestershire in 1973 and 1976 and Derbyshire in 1978.
H Walter Hammond of Gloucestershire.
I 1968 – the most notable signings being Clive Lloyd to Lancashire and Gary Sobers to Notts.
J Brian Johnston.

QUIZ 49

A Lawrence Rowe scored 214 and 100 not out for the West Indies vs New Zealand at Kingston, Jamaica, in his first Test.
B County Ground, New Writtle Street, Chelmsford.
C Worcestershire. The county only played a handful of first-class matches in 1919.
D Ole Mortensen, who was born in Vejle. He made his Derbyshire début in 1983, having previously played for Denmark.
E Alan Lilley hit 100 not out in the second innings of his début match for Essex (vs Notts at Trent Bridge in 1978).
F Geoff Humpage of Warwickshire, adding 470 with Kallicharran, against Lancashire at Southport in 1982.
G D.S. De Silva of Sri Lanka, who actually celebrated his thirty-ninth birthday during the match versus England.
H 1983.
I Jack Hobbs the Surrey cricketer.
J Basil d'Oliveira and his son Damian d'Oliveira, the latter started his career in 1982.

QUIZ 50

A   Clyde Walcott of the West Indies, versus Australia in 1954–55; 126 and 110 at Port of Spain and 155 and 110 at Kingston.

B   Birmingham. The ground was laid out in 1884.

C   Cheshire.

D   A ball delivered by a slow left-arm bowler that breaks to leg.

E   George Headley, who averaged 60.83 in twenty-two Tests.

F   Yes, run out.

G   Wills Trophy, instituted in 1977–78.

H   Ian Craig, who led Australia vs South Africa in 1957–58 aged twenty-two.

I   India's first victory was the Fifth Test at Madras in 1951–52, when Mankad took twelve wickets and India won by an innings.

J   Hall, the West Indian fast bowler from Barbados, who played in Tests from 1958–59 to 1968–69.

QUIZ 51

A   R.G. Pollock scored 274 vs Australia at Durban in 1969–70.

B   Scarborough.

C   Ken Suttle of Sussex appeared in 423 consecutive games between 1954 and 1969.

D   Australia in thirteen Tests, 1957–58 to 1960–61.

E   Maurice Leyland hit 187 and Joe Hardstaff 169 not out.

F   Four feet.

G   Glamorgan, Leicestershire and Worcestershire.

H   1966 vs West Indies, Mike Smith led England in the First Test, Colin Cowdrey in the Second, Third and Fourth, and Brian Close in the Fifth.

I   Mankad – correct name Mulwantrai Himatlal Mankad. He played for India in forty-four Tests 1946 to 1958–59 and was their leading all-rounder.

J   George Charles Downton played eight matches for Kent in 1948.

QUIZ 52

A   Allan Rae of Jamaica and Jeff Stollmeyer of Trinidad.

B   Portsmouth, it is used by Hampshire for county matches.

C Never. However, they have come third five times, the last being in 1981.
D N.B.F. Mann, who toured England with the South African sides of 1947 and 1951, heading the bowling averages in Tests on both visits.
E He played one game for Gloucestershire in 1965.
F Forward short leg.
G 1982.
H Graham Yallop vs England at Brisbane, 1978–79.
I A competition in India between five Zones – North, South, East, West and Central – into which the Ranji Trophy sides are divided.
J Graham Johnson.

QUIZ 53

A 758 for 8 declared vs West Indies at Kingston in 1954–55.
B At Headingley vs West Indies in 1957.
C C.G. Macartney hit 345 on the first day of the match between the Australians and Notts at Trent Bridge in 1921.
D Jim Laker in 1956 took 10 for 53 for England vs Australia in Old Trafford and also 10 for 88 for Surrey vs Australia at The Oval.
E Graham Gooch of Essex hit 2,559 runs, average 67.34, in 1984.
F R.W. Taylor of Derbyshire achieved 1,646 dismissals, 1,471 catches and 175 stumpings. His career lasted from 1960 to 1984.
G Prudential Assurance.
H Don Bradman in 1948.
I Imperial Cricket Conference.
J He played for Zimbabwe, having been born there in 1959.

QUIZ 54

A Australia won the series three matches to nil, but the English authorities stated that the Ashes were not at stake.
B Phillips hit a ball bowled by Edmonds on to the instep of Lamb from whence it rebounded into the hands of Gower. Phillips was judged out and that freak dismissal enabled England to win the match.
C The county club has reached its hundredth year.
D Dennis Lillee with 6 for 26 and 5 for 139.

E   G.N. Yallop in the matches between Australia and the
    West Indies in 1977–78.
F   To help in quelling a riot.
G   65 overs – the present regulations for the NatWest Trophy
    allow 60.
H   S. Venkataraghavan.
I   C.B. Fry, who played for Sussex and Hampshire.
J   Both cricketers were over the age of fifty.

QUIZ 55

A   In the members' enclosure.
B   Durban in the First Test, England winning by two wickets.
C   The Championship title was shared in both years.
D   H.J. Tayfield, the South African bowler.
E   Most Test match runs in a career.
F   Greg Chappell of Australia, 122 in eighty-seven Tests.
G   1986, when they beat Lancashire by seven wickets.
H   Imran Khan and Javed Miandad.
I   He was a lob bowler.
J   Peter Lever.

QUIZ 56

A   He created a record by hitting 114 and taking 13 for 106, in
    the Test match between England and India, which
    celebrated the Jubilee.
B   They were batting in their home town of St John's, Antigua.
C   C.J.P.G. Van Zyl of Orange Free State.
D   Rodney Hogg who took forty-one wickets.
E   Mike Smith of England was given run out when he thought
    the ball was dead and was gardening. The South African
    captain persuaded the umpire to reverse his decision.
F   This was the total number of extras given away by
    Pakistan in the three matches.
G   He held the Hampshire individual batting record for all
    three one-day competitions.
H   The selectors had appointed Brian Close as captain, but
    then sacked him, owing to controversy in the Yorks vs
    Warwicks match at Edgbaston in 1967.
    Sir C. Aubrey Smith captained England and later became
    a well-known Hollywood film star.
    Gordon Greenidge, who was playing for the West Indies
    vs India.

QUIZ 57

A   Geoff Boycott – he then joined the English team in South Africa.

B   The only two venues where Test matches have been tied.

C   They created a new Derbyshire tenth wicket record of 132 vs Yorkshire at Sheffield.

D   Neil Foster, who took twenty-nine wickets, at an average of 22.58.

E   Ramon Subba Row scored 300 vs Surrey at The Oval in 1958 – he had previously played for Surrey.

F   Rodney Marsh in 1976–77 vs England at Melbourne.

G   It created a new individual batting record for one-day internationals.

H   Jeremy Coney.

I   Wales.

J   Jim Parks of Sussex.

QUIZ 58

A   The death of Ken Barrington, who was England's assistant manager.

B   Dacca, now in Bangladesh, previously a Pakistan Test centre.

C   Michael Holding the West Indies fast bowler played for Lancashire in 1981.

D   Gladstone Small with twelve wickets, average 15.00.

E   He passed Bradman's aggregate of 6,996 runs to become Australia's leading run-scorer and took his 121st catch in Test cricket – one more than Colin Cowdrey the previous record-holder.

F   Missiles were being thrown by spectators – Clarke picked one up and threw it back, hitting a spectator in the process.

G   Glenn Turner.

H   Phil Carrick succeeded David Bairstow.

I   The Bombay Tournament, which began in 1892–93.

J   John Snow of Sussex.

QUIZ 59

A   South Africa vs England.

B   At Calcutta in protest against India's slow batting. Play was

held up while the field was cleared of unwanted fruit.
C   Gloucestershire, he made his county début in 1986.
D   Lance Gibbs, playing for West Indies versus Australia.
E   S.M.H. Kirmani with 101 not out.
F   Warren Hegg and John Stanworth – Hegg appeared in thirteen first-class matches and Stanworth in twelve.
G   Ken Higgs.
H   Graham Gooch.
I   George Hirst hit 111 and 117 not out and took 6 for 70 and 5 for 45 for Yorkshire vs Somerset at Bath in 1906.
J   A.C.S. Pigott.

QUIZ 60

A   An innings and 579 runs by England vs Australia at The Oval in 1938.
B   Dunedin, New Zealand, the first Test being staged there in 1954–55.
C   Alan Walker achieved this feat, unique in first-class cricket for Notts vs Leicestershire in 1956.
D   J.P. Agnew took 9 for 70 vs Kent at Leicester.
E   Glenn Turner.
F   Yes.
G   Chris Broad.
H   D.W. Gregory.
    Sheffield Shield.
    The sweep.

QUIZ 61

A   Khalid Ibadulla, the Warwickshire batsman, who scored 166 for Pakistan vs Australia at Karachi in 1964–65.
B   Melbourne.
C   Schweppes – this firm sponsored the County Championship from 1977 to 1983.
D   Roberts, the West Indian fast bowler, who also played for Hampshire and Leicestershire.
E   A.A. Baig, playing for India vs England at Manchester.
    Lord's. The stand is named after Sir Pelham Warner, the former England and Middlesex captain.
G   Dennis Amiss of Warwickshire.
H   Yes, versus Australia at Sydney in 1974–75. Denness, the official touring team captain, stood down due to poor batting form.

I   Essex, from 1962 to 1964 in thirty matches.
J   Maroon.

QUIZ 62

A   Richie Benaud of Australia. When he retired in 1963–64 he had hit 2,201 runs and taken 248 wickets.
B   Grace Road.
C   Alan and Colin Wells.
D   Tyrone Merrick from Antigua.
E   Mansoor Akhtar, who scored 1,156 runs, at an average of 55.04.
F   Sir Arthur Conan Doyle played for the MCC in first-class matches from 1900 to 1907.
G   Chris Old.
H   Keith Fletcher of Essex.
I   Oxford University vs Cambridge University. It has been played in every first-class season since 1838.
J   They are all double internationals, having played both rugby and cricket for their country.

QUIZ 63

A   West Indies in 1955–56.
B   Sydney and Old Trafford.
C   Kent and Yorkshire shared the title.
D   Alan Ward of Derbyshire was sent home injured before the Test series had even started.
E   Brian Irvine.
F   Bert Oldfield, who was hit on the head by a fast ball from Larwood.
G   Jack Simmons, the Lancashire cricketer.
H   Bandula Warnapura.
I   Frank Chester, who played for Worcestershire from 1912 to 1914. He umpired in Tests until 1955.
J   Australia.
ic

QUIZ 64

A   Bob Barber of Lancashire and Warwickshire.
B   McLean Park, Napier.
C   Viv Richards with 322 vs Warwickshire at Taunton.
D   Roly Jenkins for Worcestershire vs Surrey in 1949.

E Robin Hobbs vs Australians at Chelmsford.
F George Dawkes the bowler being Les Jackson vs Worcestershire.
G Desmond Haynes.
H Norman Yardley, the Yorkshire captain.
I 1864, prior to that the arm could not be raised above the shoulder.
J John Arlott.

QUIZ 65

A Colin Cowdery resumed his innings with his broken wrist in plaster. There were two balls to go, and England needed 5 runs to win with their last pair at the wicket. David Allen successfully negotiated the final deliveries and the match ended in a memorable draw.

B The Oval, 1945. Troops removed the barbed wire fences that were erected when the ground was requisitioned in 1939 for use as a prisoner-of-war enclosure. Actually, it was never put to use for this purpose, although search-lights operated from it.

C They both scored quadruple centuries. (a) Archie MacLaren – Lancashire vs Somerset, 1895 and (b) Graeme Hick – Worcestershire vs Somerset, 1988.

D (a) 'Sonny' Ramadhin and (b) Alfred Valentine. In the English summer of 1950 they took 258 wickets between them and played a decisive part in the West Indies' first Test series victory in England.

E Richard Hadlee dashes off the ground having scored 70 not out at Lord's to clinch the NatWest Trophy final for Notts in 1987.

F Denis Compton (left) and Bill Edrich of Middlesex and England.

G The Australians are celebrating their 1987 Reliance World Cup victory in Calcutta. In the picture are (left to right) *back row*: T.B.A. May, T.M. Moody, G.C. Dyer, B.A. Reid, D.C. Boon, P.L. Taylor, A.K. Zeser. *Front row*: D.M. Jones, A.R. Border, G.R. Marsh.

H Asif Iqbal (Pakistan) and Mike Denness (England). Both were born outside the countries they captained: Asif at Hyderabad, India, and Denness at Bellshill, Scotland.

I The Aborigine team that played a series of exhibition matches in England in 1868. They were the first team from Australia to tour the mother country, preceding the first team by European descent by ten years.

J Chris Broad hits his stumps over after being bowled by Steve Waugh in the Bicentennial Test, Australia vs England, at Sydney in 1988.